Seminary Motto:
The Whole Gospel for the Whole World through Whole Persons

Seminary Hymn:
All Hail the Power of Jesus' Name

Seminary Verse:
John 14:6

PRAISE & PROMISE

A PICTORIAL HISTORY OF

THE EASTERN BAPTIST THEOLOGICAL SEMINARY

BY
RANDALL L. FRAME

THE
DONNING COMPANY
PUBLISHERS

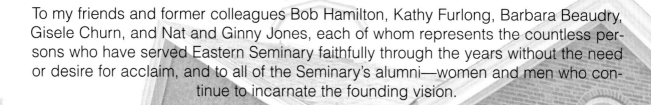

To my friends and former colleagues Bob Hamilton, Kathy Furlong, Barbara Beaudry, Gisele Churn, and Nat and Ginny Jones, each of whom represents the countless persons who have served Eastern Seminary faithfully through the years without the need or desire for acclaim, and to all of the Seminary's alumni—women and men who continue to incarnate the founding vision.

The Donning Company/Publishers
184 Business Park Drive, Suite 106
Virginia Beach, VA 23462

Steve Mull, General Manager
Mary Taylor, Project Director
Dawn V. Kofroth, Assistant General Manager
Richard A. Horwege, Senior Editor
Kelly M. Perkoski, Senior Graphic Designer
John Harrell, Imaging Artist

Library of Congress Cataloging-in-Publication Data

Frame, Randall L.
    Praise and promise : a pictorial history of the Eastern Baptist Theological Seminary / by Randall L. Frame.
        p. cm.
    Includes index.
    ISBN 1-57864-096-2 (alk. paper)
    1. Eastern Baptist Theological Seminary—History. 2. Baptist theological seminaries—Pennsylvania—History. I. Title.

BV4070.E27 F73 2000
230'.07'36174811—dc21   99-089240

Printed in the United States of America

Contents

Preface

A scene near the conclusion of the classic movie *Schindler's List* features the title character overcome with grief from the tragedy of the Holocaust. Driven to tears, Mr. Schindler is haunted by the realization that, despite all he had done to save innocent lives, he could have done more.

In preparing this history of Eastern Baptist Theological Seminary upon the occasion of its seventy-fifth anniversary, I found myself identifying at some level with the scene just described. Because so many of the Seminary's values—in the past as well as the present—represent my own values, it was inevitable that telling its history would become an emotional experience, a "labor of love" as it were. As I approached (and then passed) my deadline, I found myself regretting that I had not done more.

During the period in which I worked most intensely on this project, I noticed the pattern of each of my conversations with others somehow being directed toward the history of Eastern Seminary, often against the will of my fellow conversants. One morning I awoke at 6:00 a.m., spent most of the day poring through documents in the Seminary Archive Room, and lay wide awake at 2:00 a.m. the next day with thoughts of the Seminary's past still racing through my brain. I realized then that the time had come, whether or not I felt ready, to turn this screaming child loose. Yes, I could have done more. One can always do more. I hope I have done enough.

While I hope that scholars will find something of value in this volume, it is not intended as a critical scholarly work. Not providing careful documentation of each statement goes against my every instinct, given my background as a journalist. To have done so, however, would have made this volume far more cumbersome than it is meant to be. Readers will have to trust that I did not make anything up, and that if they spend as much time as I did in the Archive Room, they will most likely eventually find what I found. I will, however, acknowledge that at points here and there—including in instances where sources conflicted with one another or where the "facts" somehow did not add up—I had to make the best educated guess possible. In this regard, both I and the Seminary welcome corrections to, clarifications of, and additions to the historical record.

Following are the major sources for the information contained herein. As will be obvious from the text, Austen K. de Blois's *The Making of Ministers*, published in 1936, and the 1960 book *What God Hath Wrought*, edited by Gilbert Guffin, were extremely valuable in reconstructing the Seminary's early years.

Much of the content in this volume is drawn from the Seminary's official publications, including catalogues, yearbooks, and official newsletters such as *The Eastern Baptist Bulletin*, *The Easterner*, *Eastern's World*, and *inMinistry*. I also had access to the minutes taken at Board meetings through the years.

I should mention as an aside that poring through all these sources introduced something of a mystery related to the Seminary's motto that I was unable to solve. The Seminary insignia, or seal, which appears for the first time on the cover of the 1928 edition of *The Bulletin* (catalog), contains the words (in Greek) "The Whole Gospel for the Whole World." It is commonly understood that this motto reflects the Seminary's dual commitments to both the social and spiritual ramifications of the gospel. Try as I did, however, I was unable to uncover any details surrounding the origin of this motto or the specific rationale behind it.

Finally, I conducted numerous interviews with people from the Seminary's present and past, son e of whom go all the way back to the early years on Rittenhouse Square. I have chosen not to list their names so as not to draw attention to the many who could have been interviewed but were not.

Two names I must mention, however, are those of Esther George and Professor Tom McDaniel, both of whom provided extensive practical assistance as well as encouragement.

In closing, I hope that reading this illustrated history of Eastern Seminary will prove inspirational both to the Seminary's longtime friends and to its new acquaintances, even as telling the story has inspired me. I feel honored to have had the opportunity to play a part, small though it may be, in the life of this institution, whose past, albeit imperfect, is worthy of praise and whose future is bright with promise.

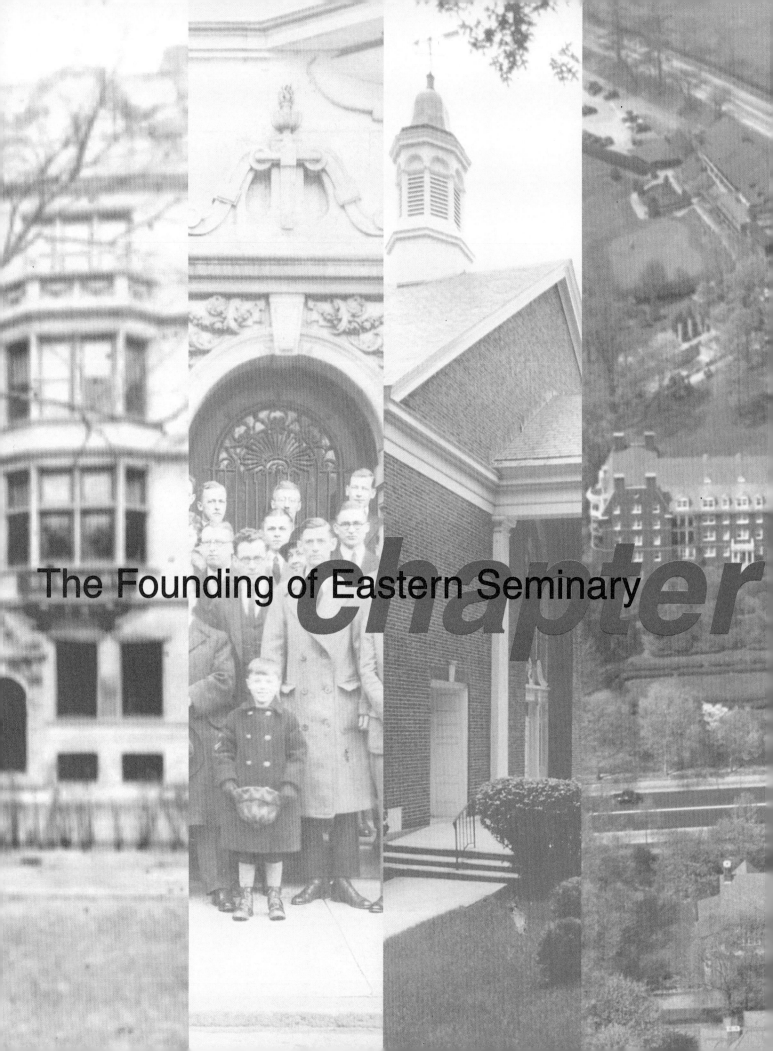

The Founding of Eastern Seminary

Any responsible telling of the history of the Eastern Baptist Theological Seminary must begin not with the official incorporation of the Seminary in March of 1925, but with a discussion of the social and theological winds that were blowing at the time. In fact, those winds began to blow in the latter part of the nineteenth century.

It was an era rife with landmark sociological developments, most notably Darwinism and the Industrial Revolution. It was also a period during which Bible scholars began to question long-held assumptions and convictions regarding the nature of Scripture and its authority. As a result, philosophical and theological foundations that had served the church and the society for centuries began to show cracks.

Some sought to repair those cracks, trying to restore the foundations to their previous state. Others, under the flag of theological liberalism, sought new foundations in which to root their religious faith. Still others questioned the very existence of meaningful foundations. While World War I was raging overseas, a battle between so-called fundamentalists and so-called modernists was raging at home in the United States.

Much of the groundwork for what church historians have labeled the "fundamentalist-modernist controversy" had been laid in a series of twelve booklets called *The Fundamentals*, published between 1909 and 1915. Only a handful of Baptists of any stripe contributed to these publications.

The advantage of describing this struggle in terms of "fundamentalists versus modernists" is that it provides a convenient framework through which to understand in general terms the issues that divided the church—both theological scholars and people in the pews—during this time. This convenient framework, however, is invoked at the risk of oversimplification.

In some ways, the world has not changed much in seventy-five years. Given the ideological extremists on both sides of current political, social, and theological issues, it is not hard to imagine the kinds of hardened ideologues who were present on both sides of the fundamentalist-modernist controversy some eight decades ago. Then, as now, it was often the extremists—as over against moderate voices in each camp—who enjoyed more success when it came to defining the terms of the debate and to garnering public attention. This reality tends to mask the fact that many during that time found themselves identifying at points with each of the predominant theological camps.

Understanding this dynamic is crucial if one is to grasp in full the motivation of those who founded Eastern Baptist Theological Seminary. For while it must be stated that ultimately the Seminary was founded in order to counter the effects of theological liberalism in both educational and church circles, it must also be stated that the Seminary's founders, as we shall see, quite consciously put distance between themselves and ultraconservative extremists, who, despite some overlapping points of agreement, were hot in pursuit of their own, distinct agenda.

THE FIRST FUNDAMENTALISTS

CURTIS LEE LAWS WAS A LEADING FIGURE IN THE EARLY FUNDAMENTALIST MOVEMENT. IN FACT IT WAS ON HIS RECOMMENDATION THAT THE MOVEMENT ADOPTED THE TERM FUNDAMENTALIST.

For the record, Eastern Seminary was founded by Fundamentalists, for that is what they called themselves. However, as Norman Maring observed in *What God Hath Wrought*, "There is little resemblance between the original Northern Baptist 'fundamentalists' and the stereotype of fundamentalism which now prevails."

These words, published by Judson Press in 1960, are just as true today. In fact, those who first took on the name *Fundamentalist* eighty years ago were in many ways the moderates of their time.

The term *Fundamentalist* owes its origins to the 1920 conference "The Fundamentals of Our Baptist Faith," held in Buffalo. Over one hundred people gathered to discuss possible responses to modernism and to the unbridled theological liberalism that accompanied it. Not long afterward, Dr. Curtis Lee Laws, for whom the Eastern Seminary chapel building would one day be named, proposed that those who were part of this movement adopt for themselves the term *Fundamentalist*.

The original Fundamentalists, as Maring observed, "were moderates both in theological position and in temperament." The few extremists who attended the 1920 Buffalo conference eventually left the movement because it was not radical enough for them. Many such persons found representation in a group called the Bible Union, organized in 1923. Spokesmen for the Bible Union typically accused Fundamentalists of being traitors to the cause against liberalism.

Those within the Bible Union movement tended to dismiss wholesale any scholarly criticism that might call into question traditional interpretations or theories of interpretation of Scripture. In addition, they placed opposition to the theory of evolution at the top of their agenda alongside such emphases as the infallibility of the Scriptures, the Virgin Birth, substitutionary atonement, and the resurrection and pre-millennial return of Jesus Christ.

Fundamentalists, in contrast, were open to scholarly criticism of the Bible so long as it was done with reverence, that is, for the purpose of clarifying and building faith as opposed to destroying it. As Dr. Augustus H. Strong, a representative of early Fundamentalist views, put it, "Higher criticism has its rights, and instead of denouncing it, we must concede that it has thrown valuable light upon the methods employed in the composition of the Scripture."

For Fundamentalists, the ultimate battle was not over particular theories of inspiration or secondary doctrines. Instead it was a battle between the radical rationalism of modernity and the supernaturalism of Christian faith. Fundamentalists focused, according to Maring, on "the ultimate question as to whether or not God had really spoken a saving word in Jesus Christ."

Thus, theories of inspiration and secondary doctrines were open to debate. In contrast, affirmation of the saving work of Jesus Christ and of the Bible's unique status in testifying to that saving work were not so open.

Because they viewed the Bible as God's revelation pertaining to salvation and not as a scientific textbook, the first Fundamentalists did not make an issue of evolutionary theory per se, so long as it was viewed as being compatible with theism, and thus with faith. As Dr. Laws wrote, "We do not ask [the Bible] about chemistry or astronomy or the constitution of matter, or the expansive power of gases, just as we do not ask a compass to tell us the time of the day, or predict the weather."

Likewise, Laws and other leaders within the movement stated on more than one occasion that while Fundamentalists believed in the actual return of Christ, they were not tied to premillennialism, postmillennialism, or any other particular view.

According to Dr. Frank M. Goodchild, the first chairman of Eastern Seminary's Board of Trustees, the five defining points of Fundamentalism were as follows:

"(1)We believe that the Bible is God's Word. (2)Fundamentalists believe just as strongly in the church as in the Bible. (3)Fundamentalists believe in the denomination. (4)Fundamentalists believe in schools. (5)Fundamentalists believe thoroughly in missions."

As suggested by these five points, Fundamentalists aspired to reform their denomination from within, whereas more radical forces talked of secession from what was known then as the Northern Baptist Convention (NBC).

Upholding the Essentials of the Faith

Fundamentalists' efforts to distance themselves from their more conservative brethren, however, should not mask their deep concerns about the faith-destroying effects of radical theological liberalism. They were particularly concerned about seminaries and colleges within the

Northern Baptist Convention because of the strong influence educational institutions wielded on the life and thought of the church.

After the 1920 Buffalo Convention, those who had convened the meeting selected a committee to investigate the denomination's schools and to issue a report the following year. Dr. Goodchild chaired the committee, among whose members was Dr. Austen Kennedy de Blois, who would later play a crucial role in Eastern Seminary's formative years as the Seminary's second president.

The committee's report on the schools was not nearly so negative as some had thought (and perhaps even hoped) it would be. Despite some problems, the committee expressed confidence "that for the most part our schools of all grades are doing a work of which the denomination may well be proud."

Tensions were reignited, however, as a result of a movement in the early 1920s to urge the NBC to pass a doctrinal statement. Against the advice of moderates, who believed that more careful planning was needed, impetuous conservative firebrands pressed for immediate action. Their efforts failed. Afterwards, the Convention adopted a resolution that read as follows: "That the Northern Baptist Convention affirm that the New Testament is an all-sufficient ground for Baptist faith and practice, and they need no other statement."

In this same period, during which enrollment in Northern Baptist Convention seminaries was in decline, various scholars within church ranks were writing articles and books ridiculing conservative beliefs and espousing some of the key tenets of modernism and theological liberalism. A small group of Fundamentalists determined that liberalism could not be held in check in the denomination's older institutions. And they wanted a better alternative to the Bible schools that were springing up across the land as a response to liberalism.

THE FOUNDING OF EASTERN SEMINARY

While many were talking about the need for a conservative seminary, two men in particular—Rev. L. W. Barnard and Rev. Charles T. Ball—were committed to taking action. Barnard organized a meeting in New York for November 18, 1924, to discuss the creation of a chain of Bible colleges to be overseen by a parent institution that would include a theological seminary.

Charles T. Ball, pastor of the Wissinoming Baptist Church in Philadelphia, had long been interested in the theological training of young people. His primary interest was to establish a Baptist theological seminary in the North, following the general model of Southwestern Baptist Seminary in Fort Worth, Texas, where he had previously taught.

At the November meeting, at which only eight men (including Ball and Barnard) were present, Rev. Gordon H. Baker proposed that a Baptist seminary be organized in Philadelphia. Those present constituted themselves as the Board of Trustees for the projected institution, and Dr. Frank M. Goodchild was elected president.

Meanwhile, differences of opinion arose between the Reverends Ball and Barnard, the latter of whom disassociated himself from the movement. The idea of a chain of Bible colleges was dropped, and the focus of those who remained turned toward establishing a seminary.

On February 16, 1925, four men—Charles Ball, Harry Watson Barras, Ralph Mayberry, and John A. Hainer—constituted themselves as an executive committee and called for a meeting, to be held on March 19, 1925, for the purpose of organizing a Baptist seminary. They did so despite the widely held sentiment that eight theological seminaries and two missionary training schools were more than enough for the denomination.

At 2:00 p.m. on March 19, 1925, six men—all of them ministers—gathered at 1701 Chestnut Street in Philadelphia, the headquarters of the American Baptist Publication Society. On that historic day, Charles T. Ball, Harry Watson Barras, Groves W. Drew, Ralph L. Mayberry, John A. Hainer, and Gordon H. Baker held the constituting meeting for the Eastern Baptist Theological Seminary.

All but Dr. Drew agreed to act as trustees. Others selected that day to serve as charter Board of Trustees members were James A. Maxwell,

GORDON H. BAKER, A PASTOR FROM SCHENECTADY, NEW YORK, WAS AMONG THE SIX FOUNDERS OF EASTERN SEMINARY. HE SERVED ON THE BOARD FROM ITS INCEPTION UNTIL HIS DEATH IN 1963.

CHARLES T. BALL, THE FIRST PRESIDENT OF EASTERN SEMINARY, WAS KNOWN AS A MAN OF ACTION AND A HIGHLY SKILLED PROMOTER.

David Lee Jamison, Frank Earle Parham, John E. Briggs, Curtis Lee Laws, Frank M. Goodchild, and Thornley B. Wood. Dr. Goodchild was elected chairman of the Board, and Rev. Charles T. Ball was chosen as the Seminary's first president. Later in the year several others were added to the Board: P. Vanis Slawter, E. B. Dwyer, William P. Haug, Ralph I. Levering, Wesley H. Hoot, William H. Waite, Henry W. Munger, John B. Champion, Lawrence N. Sirrell, Joseph Y. Erwin, Mrs. Carl R. Gray, and Alonzo R. Stark.

The essential goal of the founders was to represent in the arena of seminary education a sane and healthy conservatism. In the June 18, 1925 issue of *The Watchman-Examiner*, a national Baptist paper with headquarters in New York City, Dr. Laws, its editor, set forth with eloquence the rationale for the new institution:

"We have voiced our protest against certain teachings again and again. We propose to do it no more. Those in charge of the new seminary propose founding a school of the prophets in which loyalty to the Scriptures shall be conspicuous. You will not get the impression when you visit its classrooms that they are cutting to pieces that Book that brought you the good news of your salvation and has been the unfailing source of your comfort and inspiration for many years. You will not come away feeling that the crown of deity has been taken off the brow of the One whom your soul adores."

The founders, true to the values and principles they had espoused as conservatives in the years leading up to the Seminary's founding, made it clear they did not belong in the camp of ultraconservative extremists. As Maring put it, "It was their intention to establish an institution in which the essential elements of the Christian faith would be preserved, and which at the same time would represent an enlightened scholarship. Indeed, it may be fairly stated that the founders hoped to institute a school which would be conservative and progressive at the same time."

These values were reflected in the Doctrinal Basis that served to outline the Seminary's guiding theological values. The statement's affirmations addressed the essential tenets of Christian faith. Except for the

---

We believe that the Bible, composed of the Old and New Testaments, is inspired of God, and is of supreme and final authority in faith and life.

We believe in the supernatural as the vital element in the revelation and operation of the Christian Faith.

We believe in one God eternally existing in three Persons—Father, Son, and Holy Spirit.

We believe that man was created in the image of God, and that he sinned, and thereby incurred spiritual death.

We believe that Jesus Christ was begotten of the Holy Spirit and born of the virgin Mary, and that He is true God and true man, and is the only and sufficient Mediator between God and man.

We believe in the vicarious death of the Lord Jesus Christ for our sins, in the resurrection of His body, His ascension into Heaven; and that salvation is received only through personal faith in Him.

We believe in the personality of the Holy Spirit and that His ministry is to reveal Christ to men in the regeneration and sanctification of their souls.

We believe that baptism is immersion of a believer in water, in the name of the Father, and of the Son, and of the Holy Spirit; setting forth the essential facts in redemption—the death and resurrection of Christ; also essential facts in the experience of the believer—death to sin and resurrection to newness of life.

We believe that a New Testament church is a body of believers thus baptized, associated for worship, service, the spread of the Gospel, and the establishing of the Kingdom in all the world.

We believe . . . that the Lord's Supper is a commemoration of the Lord's death until He comes.

Since its inception, the Doctrinal Basis has been signed annually by faculty and by members of the Seminary's Board of Trustees. It has undergone only slight revisions, some of which were designed to make the language gender-neutral. In the early 1980s, provisions were made for non-Baptists who might not subscribe to the statement's views on baptism.

specifically Baptist views on baptism, the statement in essence was nothing more than what the Church had affirmed for centuries, including the vicarious atonement of Christ, the authority of Scriptures, and the return of Christ, though the statement does not commit to any specific millennial position.

From the wording of the original Doctrinal Basis, it is evident that it emerged during a time when the very foundations of historic Christian faith were being doubted or denied.

IRENIC DEMEANOR

By and large, those who gave birth and life to Eastern Seminary were thoughtful, caring men, magnanimous of spirit. They treated all people, including those with whom they disagreed, with decency and respect. Often their courtesy was returned. In 1926, the year Dr. Austen K. de Blois left his post as co-editor of *The Watchman-Examiner* to become president of Eastern Seminary, an editorial writer in a leading Unitarian periodical called him "a man of grace and charm, of dignity and scholarship." This, despite the fact that the writer vehemently disagreed with de Blois and his colleagues on virtually all of the major doctrinal issues of the day.

Drs. de Blois, Laws, Goodchild, and others were known for their ability to disagree without being disagreeable, to challenge without being caustic or unkind. Maring notes that the Seminary's founders were by no means monolithic with regard to their personalities or their theological viewpoints. But notably absent in those early days were such leaders as Drs. W. B. Riley, J. Frank Norris, and T. T. Shields, widely regarded as extremists both by supporters and detractors.

The six who gathered on March 19, 1925, could barely imagine the results their meeting would produce. As Ralph Mayberry put it in 1974, "We started out not knowing where we were going or whether we were going." The founders and the many others who would soon join them had next to no financial resources, no buildings, no books or supplies. They did, however, have a vision, one that they firmly believed was grounded in the will of God. And they were ready to go to work, to commit the time and energy required to see their vision through to reality, emboldened with confidence that what they had was more important than what they did not have. Seventy-five years worth of fruitful history have proved them correct.

"Conservative, yet progressive." "In pursuit of a healthy and sane conservatism." These are the primary phrases that capture the ideals that served as a basis for the founding of Eastern Seminary. These values continue to define Eastern Seminary at the dawn of the third millennium.

RALPH L. MAYBERRY, SHOWN HERE IN HIS LATER YEARS, WAS THE LAST OF THE SIX FOUNDERS TO PASS AWAY (IN 1980).

A Remarkable First Year *chapter*

No matter what the circumstances, launching a seminary is a daunting task, to say the least. It is particularly daunting when starting from scratch: no money, no buildings, no books or supplies.

Much of the human credit for the Seminary's productive inaugural year belongs to its first president, Charles Ball, considered by some to be a genius when it came to promotional ability. But virtually all trustees and other supporters played significant roles. Almost every Sunday Dr. Harry Watson Barras visited churches to describe the new school's mission and request support. The first financial gift to the Seminary came from Blockley Baptist Church in Philadelphia, where Rev. John A. Hainer was pastor. William J. Hand, whose association with the Seminary spans six decades, including over twenty-five years as librarian, was a young boy at Blockley Baptist and still remembers his pastor's appeal on behalf of the new seminary. The amount was $26, not quite enough for a healthy endowment but a start. In fact, its purpose was to cover the $25 cost of a charter.

Most churches, though supportive of the Seminary's mission, were not in a position to make major financial gifts. Undaunted, the Seminary's leaders proceeded as if the money would come. An eight-page bulletin announcing the founding of the new Seminary was mailed to ten thousand addresses around the country. One of the bulletins ended up in the hands of a wealthy couple on the West Coast.

At a Board meeting on May 28, 1925, barely two months after the Seminary had been incorporated, Dr. James A. Maxwell amazed trustees with the announcement that a man from California and his wife had made a gift of twenty thousand shares of stock, worth more than $500,000. Furthermore, they promised there would be more to follow. The gift came with the message that the Seminary must remain true to its founding mission and that the source of the gift must remain a secret or "it is all off."

Dr. Gordon Baker would later write:

"I shall never forget the moment when the gift was announced. A holy hush fell on the meeting. Our first act was to engage in prayers of thanksgiving and dedication. There was profound gratitude in all our hearts, and with it a sense of grave responsibility that prevented any outward demonstration of joy."

The original plan called for classes to be held in a Sunday school room at a Philadelphia church. Local pastors would be recruited to serve as part-time teachers. A room at the Publication Society would serve as headquarters for the Seminary. They projected a student body for the first year of between twelve and fifteen. (Amazingly, it would reach to over one hundred.)

With the arrival of the unanticipated financial resources, plans changed drastically. The trustees purchased a building on South Rittenhouse Square in Philadelphia that became the original location of Eastern Seminary. Soon after, they bought a second building on the Square. Nine full-time professors and six additional instructors (three of whom were women) were recruited to teach. In July of 1925 the Board adopted a budget of $30,000 a year for salaries, setting the salary for full-time professors at $3,600.

Amidst the positive developments, however, there were also some tensions. Reading between the lines of Austen Kennedy de Blois's account in *The Making of Ministers*, one can conclude that there were differences of opinion as to whether the new seminary should be led by Rev. Charles Ball or Dr. Frank Goodchild. Tensions arose between the two men, resulting, much to the dismay of many Board members, in the disassociation from the Seminary of the highly respected Dr. Goodchild on September 10, 1925. Early Board minutes make reference to a two-person committee dispatched to try to change his mind, but he said his decision was final. Dr. Goodchild, however, would later donate many volumes from his library to the Seminary.

Given the odds against this nascent seminary, the story of its first year is almost too spectacular to believe. It is no wonder that to those familiar with its story, Eastern Baptist Theological Seminary became known as the "Miracle of Faith." Over the summer, the focus had turned toward the designing of an educational philosophy and the recruiting of faculty and students. Within a week of the scheduled opening of classes, however, the school had no curriculum.

In 1974, William W. Adams, who chaired the original Curriculum Committee, recalled meeting Charles Ball for the first time at about 11:00 a.m. on Friday, September 19, 1925. Dr. Ball gave him the assignment of drafting a curriculum over the weekend. "I don't remember

how shocked I looked," Dr. Adams recalled, "but he must have known that he had shocked me."

Dr. Adams recruited some help and went to work, getting very little sleep. He skipped church on Sunday, which for him no doubt was the modern-day equivalent of skipping game seven of the World Series. But by Monday morning, a makeshift curriculum, written in longhand, was ready to be implemented.

On September 22, 1925, the Seminary opened its doors to students with four schools: the School of Theology, the School of Religious Education, the School of Missions, and the School of Sacred Music.

THE FOUNDERS WERE CONTENT TO USE LOCAL CHURCHES FOR CLASSROOMS, BUT AN ANONYMOUS GIFT WORTH $500,000 ENABLED THE SEMINARY TO BUY A CAMPUS ON RITTENHOUSE SQUARE. SHOWN HERE ARE THE DINING HALL AND A STUDENT LIVING ROOM.

The charter faculty consisted of nine full-time professors—Charles T. Ball, Barnard C. Taylor, William W. Adams, Harry Watson Barras, David Lee Jamison, Arthur E. Harris, Wilber T. Elmore, John B. Champion, and George W. Swope—and six instructors: L. Sarle Brown, Mrs. Wilber T. Elmore, Boyce Hudson Moody, Mrs. C. Harold Thompson, Edward K. Worrell, and Grace R. Vanaman.

Curriculum Committees from both the faculty and the Board worked in harmony to refine the curriculum for each school. In his 1926 report to the Board, President Ball made reference to having made seven trips to Harrisburg. The success of all these efforts became evident when, in December of 1925, the Pennsylvania State Council of Education sent a representative from Harrisburg to examine the new school. After a thorough investigation of the class offerings, officers, faculty, trustees, and facilities, the Seminary, which eight months previous was a mere dream, was granted the authority to offer five degrees: Bachelor of Theology (B.Th.), Bachelor of Divinity (B.D.), Master of Theology (Th.M.), Doctor of Theology (Th.D.), and Doctor of Divinity (D.D.).

Students were not at first charged tuition, and had to pay only $6 a week for board and lodging. All who applied were admitted, a situation that Dr. de Blois, who held to very high academic standards, would later remedy. Though some of the Seminary's first students possessed keen powers of intellect, others were not even high school graduates, while most had not attended college. Wrote de Blois, "It is a well-known fact that almost any new educational institution can attract a large number of students, provided its conditions of entrance are not severe. It is also a notable, or shall we say

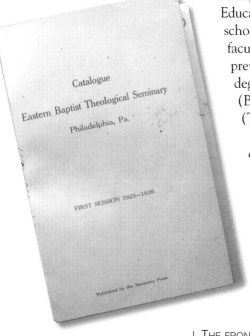

THE FRONT PAGE OF THE SEMINARY'S FIRST CATALOG. AMONG THE CLASSES OFFERED IN THAT FIRST YEAR WERE PSYCHOLOGY OF MUSICAL TALENT, CHURCH EFFICIENCY, PSYCHOLOGY OF ADOLESCENCE, AND THE CHALLENGE OF THE CITY.

notorious, fact that many men seek to enter the ministerial calling, who have failed to make good in any activity that demands a certain amount of brains and a large measure of consecrated will-power."

The Seminary's original faculty, undaunted, simply did the best they could at placing students in classes and programs that would best suit their varied educational experiences. This entailed the early establishment of a certificate program for those who came to the Seminary without the proper qualifications to pursue a graduate theological degree. In addition, no student was denied admission because he or she could not pay for a room or apartment.

Many may regard "distance education" as a contemporary concept, but it was actually in November of its first year that the Seminary began a correspondence program that in succeeding years would provide hundreds of pastors and lay workers with affordable, convenient, and quality theological training, all via the mail. In 1930, the Seminary's Correspondence Course got a boost in the form of an official endorsement from the Baptist State Convention of New York.

The task not only of teaching students but of looking after their housing and material needs, as well as maintaining the financial affairs of the Seminary, required the dedicated contributions of all those associated with getting it off the ground. While it enjoyed remarkable progress, the Seminary did not get through its first year untainted. Dr. George W. Swope, the much-beloved charter professor of Evangelism, died of a heart condition on March 17, 1926, casting a pall on the Seminary's celebration, a few days later, of its founding the previous year.

The Seminary held its first commencement in May of 1926. President Charles T. Ball delivered the address to graduates. It would be his last official act on behalf of the Seminary. Even in its first year, some students qualified for degrees because of previous work they had done. The Seminary awarded two diplomas, one Bachelor of Theology degree, two Bachelor of Divinity degrees, two Master of Theology degrees, one Doctor of Theology degree, and three Bachelor of Religious Education degrees. The conferring of an additional degree, Doctor of Religious Education, was deferred pending the authority (from the State Council of Education) to grant it.

In May of 1926, at the first annual meeting of the Board of Trustees, Finance Committee Chairman Ralph Levering reported investments of $989,140.87. Board Treasurer Harry Barras reported that churches had

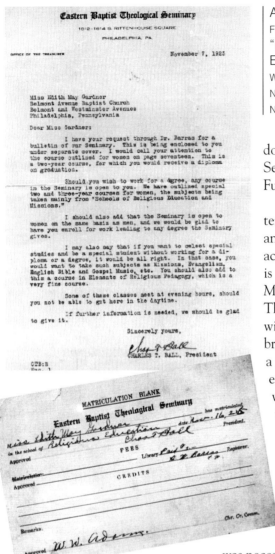

donated about $13,000 to the Seminary and that the Student Aid Fund had received over $5,000.

Beyond the above-mentioned tensions surrounding Charles Ball and Frank Goodchild, no definitive account of President Ball's departure is offered in either *The Making of Ministers* or *What God Hath Wrought*. The Seminary's founding president is widely acknowledged to have been a brilliant organizer and promoter. But a majority of Board members apparently decided that another person was needed to take the Seminary to the higher levels of accomplishment and recognition it was seeking.

Ralph Mayberry said in a 1974 interview that Dr. Ball had been "very active in promoting the new Seminary and wanted very much to be president. It was necessary for us to elect him president at the very beginning. We couldn't do otherwise. But it was also necessary to find another president."

Rev. Charles Ball was asked to remain with the Seminary in some capacity to serve as a promoter, but he declined. Meanwhile, the Seminary found the person for whom it was looking in Dr. Austin Kennedy de Blois, who at the time he was called served as associate editor of *The Watchman Examiner*. Arguably, Dr. de Blois in his ten years as president would do more to shape Eastern Seminary's mission and enhance its reputation than any other one person in its history.

The Seminary's home for its first fifteen years was on Rittenhouse Square in Philadelphia.

Members of the community posed for this photo during the first year. At the far left is Professor John B. Champion. Next to him is Professor William W. Adams. The short man front and center is Professor Arthur E. Harris. The man with the glasses behind the boy is L. Sarle Brown. Behind Harris's right shoulder is Professor David Lee Jamison. To the left of Harris is Professor Wilber T. Elmore. To Elmore's left is President Charles T. Ball. The second man to the left of President Ball is Professor Barnard C. Taylor.

President Charles T. Ball (seventh from left in front row) poses with members of the Seminary's first graduating class and others in 1926.

The Formative Years

In the spring of 1926, Professor Harry Watson Barras was dispatched to New York City to confer with Curtis Lee Laws, editor of *The Watchman-Examiner*, regarding a possible successor to President Ball. According to Barras, at one point during the meeting, Dr. Laws pointed with his thumb over his right shoulder to the office behind him and said, "I have the best man in the country for this position, but you can't get him." He was referring to Dr. Austen Kennedy de Blois, co-editor of *The Watchman-Examiner*.

Board Chairman Dr. James Maxwell was undaunted. Barras would later describe Maxwell as a person "to whom obstacles are stepping-stones." Dr. Maxwell sent Professor Barras back to New York City with instructions to "attack the lion in his den." Barras was granted an interview with Dr. de Blois, who agreed to meet with the Executive Committee of the Seminary's Board.

All this took place before it was certain that President Ball would be leaving. At the May 3, 1926 Board meeting, Dr. Ball's name was placed in nomination by John Hainer, while Dr. de Blois was officially nominated by Gordon Baker. The Board chose Dr. de Blois.

For those yet uncertain about how seriously to take this upstart Philadelphia seminary, Dr. de Blois, described by Dr. Baker as "a man of scholarly habits and of wide influence far beyond Baptist circles," provided instant credibility. Dr. de Blois understood what was required to lead a Christian institution of higher learning, having served previously as president of Union Baptist Seminary in New Brunswick, Canada, and later as president of Shurtleff College in Illinois.

Dr. de Blois had written several books, including *Imperialism and Democracy* (1901), *Life of John Mason Peck* (1917), and *The Message of Wisdom: Studies in the Book of Proverbs* (1920). He had also served successfully as pastor of First Baptist Church in Chicago and of First Baptist Church in Boston. His role at *The Watchman-Examiner* testified to his abilities as a communicator. In short, his credentials for accomplishing the task at hand were virtually impeccable.

Shortly after accepting the presidency, Dr. de Blois, with the following statement, made known the values and commitments that would guide his leadership:

"My purpose in the conduct of this institution, already so highly honored of God, and prosperous, is five-fold: (1) To enthrone the English Bible at the heart of our many-sided work, central to all our studies and efforts. (2) To emphasize evangelism as the attitude and end of our teaching service and practical activities. (3) To provide complete and scholarly training in all departments of a first-class and well-rounded theological curriculum. (4) To seek constantly the direct guidance of the Holy Spirit, that the missionary passion may empower our plans and labors. (5) To serve our great denomination with unswerving loyalty."

His high stature as an academic and leader notwithstanding, the president was friendly and approachable. Culbert G. Rutenber remembers during his student years at the Seminary letting loose playing a jazz piece on the chapel piano before realizing that the president had "snuck up" behind him. The young Rutenber apologized, but President de Blois assured him it was not necessary: "We need more of that kind of thing around here."

For the first two years of his presidency, Dr. de Blois split time between Philadelphia and New York City, where he continued to make his home and serve as co-editor of *The Watchman-Examiner*. During those two years Dr. Barras served as dean, handling the Seminary's administrative chores when the president was not in.

Initially one of the new president's top priorities was to tell the story of Eastern Seminary as far and wide as he could. He did so by visiting colleges, universities, other seminaries, and churches. Several of the Seminary's early professors did the same, and as a result the Seminary's reputation as an institution of high standing and noble purpose took major strides forward. Dr. de Blois's influence no doubt went a long way toward the Seminary's gaining the recognition of the Board of Education of the Northern Baptist Convention, which resulted in the promotional benefits associated with denominational backing.

NO ONE PERSON DID MORE TO SHAPE THE SEMINARY'S MISSION AND TO ENHANCE ITS IMAGE THAN ITS SECOND PRESIDENT, AUSTEN KENNEDY DE BLOIS.

BUILDING THE FACULTY

Among the early concerns of the Seminary's founders was academic quality, or, more specifically, the lack thereof. The character and integrity of early faculty members were beyond dispute. However, some trustees and administrators felt that the qualifications of the faculty as a whole were inadequate. Only four of those who served on the faculty during the first two years had earned doctorates.

Some professors were experts in at least one or two areas of pastoral ministry or administration. But they were not equipped to enter in any significant way into the important scholarly debates of the time. So long as that was the case, the dream of an institution that would be both theologically conservative and academically strong would remain beyond reach. As Gordon Baker put it, the founders of Eastern Seminary "wanted to prove to the world that a man can be a scholar and still believe the Bible to be the word of God."

Herbert F. Stilwell, widely regarded as a man of keen intellect and lovable disposition, was brought in to replace the late Dr. Swope. Dr. Stilwell had been secretary of evangelism for the denomination's Home Mission Society and was known for his strong commitment to evangelism.

Dr. Maxwell, who in addition to serving as president of the Board of Trustees was a highly regarded scholar, accepted the call to lead the Department of English Bible during the Seminary's second year. A friend of the Seminary, most likely the same one who had earlier given $500,000 worth of stock, gave $100,000 to endow the chair that Dr. Maxwell would occupy until 1948. Dr. George F. Wortley, who had recently received a Ph.D. from Boston University, was called to lead the School of Religious Education.

Both Stilwell and Wortley resigned in 1930 and were replaced by Benjamin T. Livingston (Evangelism) and Donald R. Gorham (Religious

Education). In 1935, the name of the Department of Religious Education was changed to the Department of Christian Education.

Among the others who began teaching at the Seminary under President de Blois was Rhodes scholar Carl H. Morgan, who entered Eastern Seminary as a student in 1926. He continued his association with the Seminary while earning his Ph.D. from the University of Pennsylvania. Widely regarded as a "Renaissance man," he started teaching in the School of Sacred Music in 1927. Before long he was teaching New Testament Greek.

Dr. Morgan played a leading role in establishing the undergraduate program at the Seminary. Known originally as the Pre-Theological or Sub-Junior Department, it was formally introduced in 1932 as the Collegiate Division.

After Dr. Adams left in 1946 to become president of Central Baptist Theological Seminary in Kansas City, Dr. Morgan took his place as professor of New Testament Interpretation and Greek. Because of the influence he would have on so many students for so many years, Dr. Morgan would one day come to be known as "Mr. Eastern." Dr. Glenn Koch, who in 1969 would take over for Dr. Morgan, recalls that his mentor was a consummate scholar and first-class lecturer: "Over time, he learned what questions students were likely to ask, and so he addressed those questions before they were asked. To watch him work was magical."

Another who was destined to become one of the Seminary's most greatly loved and widely influential professors was the aforementioned Culbert G. "Cubby" Rutenber, a charter instructor in the Collegiate Division.

The Seminary from the beginning recognized the importance of Christian Education and Music for the vitality of the church and the promulgation of the gospel. The success of the program was due mainly to the talents and efforts of Dr. L. Sarle Brown and his assistant, Joseph Bowman, who in those early years led tour choirs—both male and female—up into New England and as far south as Georgia.

Dr. Austen Kennedy de Blois enthusiastically supported the emphases on Christian Education and Music. He wrote, "Although music forms so large and important a part in the services of worship, and in all the general gatherings of every church and its organizations, it is a subject that has been strangely neglected in the theological seminaries and training schools for Christian workers. So far as the Northern States are concerned, Eastern Seminary has been the pioneer in supplying this feature in present-day ministerial education."

Seminary Board member Richard Shearer, who took voice lessons under L. Sarle Brown en route to becoming a baritone soloist for the choir some sixty years ago, says he is committed today to urging the Seminary to reinstitute a music program that resembles the one it had in the beginning. "I'm still going to make that push," he says, "because Eastern Seminary does not seem right to me without good music."

JOSEPH R. BOWMAN TAUGHT MUSIC AND LED THE SEMINARY'S CHOIRS FROM 1936 TILL 1952, WHEN HE WENT ON TO SERVE AT EASTERN BAPTIST COLLEGE.

A HIGH VIEW OF SCHOLARSHIP

It is clear from his writings that Dr. de Blois bristled even at the suggestion that the Seminary was little more than a glorified Bible school. He was a man on a mission to obliterate this perception. Doing such would entail raising academic standards, as well as the standards for admission. The following statement is part of a 1928 address he gave to the Board of Trustees:

VIRGINIA SNYDER, GREATLY ADMIRED BY HER PIANO STUDENTS, TAUGHT MUSIC IN THE COLLEGIATE DIVISION FOR TWENTY-FIVE YEARS, BEGINNING IN 1929.

"The purpose of our Seminary is to compete triumphantly with the modernist theological seminaries. To do so we must meet them on their own level in the educational field. We must give just as virile an intellectual discipline. We must prepare just as accurate a scholarship, and a scholarship much more sound. We must secure for our Baptist pastorates an ever-enlarging group of thoroughly trained men who shall be loyal in all things to Jesus Christ and the fundamentals of the Christian faith, and who shall be just as able, as scholarly, as intellectually equipped, and as devoted to sinewy intellectual labors, as the men who go forth from those schools which have lost their fair vision of an atoning Savior."

The quality of students constitutes a major, recurring theme in de Blois's book *The Making of Ministers*, which consists mainly of the president's yearly reports of his tenure, written in retrospect. "The Seminary did not want second-rate students," he wrote. "In the earlier years of the School it was a difficult task to eliminate those of this class who were applicants for admission; but each student was studied carefully as an individual case, and as far as possible those who were inferior were gently but firmly eliminated, in order that they might not interfere with the progress of others." By 1930, the percentage of students coming to the Seminary who had attended college had grown to sixty-five. During the first year, it was under ten.

At Dr. de Blois's suggestion, the Seminary abolished evening classes because they allegedly attracted inferior students. Presumably for the same reason, it dropped its certificate program in the early 1930s and established a graduate program. The standards for admissions were raised, as were the academic expectations of students. During the de Blois years, the passing grade was raised from 75 to 80 percent.

In his quest for quality, Dr. de Blois was fully prepared to sacrifice numbers: "The first question a stranger always asks is 'How many students have you?' The second question almost invariably is 'How many of that number are college graduates?' Then the secret is out!"

Over six decades later, one can almost see Dr. de Blois brimming with pride when writing that in the summer of 1931, "twenty-three applications for admission were denied."

During the Seminary's fifth year, it took major steps to enhance the quality of the Master and Doctor of Theology programs. Writes Dr. de Blois, "It was decided that the record of every applicant for either of these degrees should be carefully investigated; that only students who had maintained a uniformly high standard of work during their period of

college and seminary training should be accepted as candidates; that professors offering graduate courses should require of every student regular attendance at class and seminar discussions, and a rigid system of independent research work, with frequent submission of papers and outlines; that the subject of the final thesis should be submitted during the first year of graduate study; that both written and oral examinations should be held at the close of each course; that the final thesis should display original and vital thought; and that the thesis for the degree of Th.D. should be presented and defended before the entire Faculty."

Such policies resulted in some students being advised to discontinue their studies, though the Seminary designed a four-year program (instead

To the surprise of no one, the Office of the President contained numerous books. Dr. de Blois was known as a lover of good books.

of the usual three) for students who showed ability but lacked adequate preparation.

During the 1929–30 school year, it was decided by the faculty that any student who married during the school session without faculty consent would be dropped from classes for the remainder of the academic year. But in discussing this policy, the president wrote, "The members of Eastern's Faculty have always been kind-hearted, sympathetic and long-suffering individuals; so it may be enough to add that this rule, which sounds rather drastic, has been observed with a fair degree of consistency and a modicum of heartless rigidity, but that at times the weakness of professorial benignity has prevailed over judicial severity." (This might be construed as a distinguished academic's way of saying that this policy was not strictly enforced.)

THE SEMINARY LIBRARY DURING THE DAYS ON RITTENHOUSE SQUARE.

BUILDING THE LIBRARY

It is with good reason that the Board of Trustees, when the Seminary moved to Overbrook in 1940, voted to name the library there in honor of Dr. de Blois. The president's eye for acquiring books on a skeleton budget was legendary. A lover of good books, he traveled to Europe frequently and regularly returned with hundreds of volumes. On one occasion he said, "I see no reason why, by patience and diligence, we should not gather a thoroughly representative Baptist library which will compare favorably with any in the world."

In a report to the Board early in his administration, the president confessed, "Our books are as yet styled a Library only by courtesy." He called for the addition of at least twenty-five hundred quality volumes at an estimated cost of $5,000: "This would not give us a library, but it would secure the beginning of a library, and would relieve our present embarrassments."

At the May 1929 Board meeting, the president asked for $300 to acquire books for the library. The Board gave him $1,200 instead, and the result was an additional two thousand volumes. Many of those were acquired over the summer in the bookshops of London, where the president examined over forty thousand volumes. During this time, the Seminary was also acquiring periodicals, including complete sets of *The Baptist Magazine* and *American Baptist Missionary Magazine*.

But according to the president, "a pile of books is simply a pile of lumber until a competent librarian takes charge of them." The Seminary found this competence in 1928, when Miss Eleanor Price became the

Seminary's first full-time librarian. For over ten years she brought order and efficiency to the growing library.

During the 1931–32 school year, Dr. David Lee Jamison became curator of the library, though that did not stop President de Blois from acquiring several hundred volumes each year. By the time Dr. de Blois stepped down, the library had grown to an impressive fourteen thousand volumes, most of them selected, according to the president, "with the utmost care."

CAMPUS EXPANSION

By 1930, the Seminary had 127 alumni serving as pastors in different parts of the United States and seven serving on foreign fields as missionaries. The enrollment for the 1929–30 school year reached 158. This was almost double the enrollment of other Baptist seminaries in the East, including Newton, Crozer, and Colgate-Rochester.

No student was ever turned away because of a lack of housing. But to accommodate the growth, the Seminary had to buy more buildings. During the 1926–27 school year, it purchased for $58,000 the four-story building on 1814 Spruce Street, which bordered Rittenhouse Square. It

PICTURED ARE FOURTEEN OF THE TWENTY-ONE MEMBERS OF THE CLASS OF 1927. FRONT ROW, LEFT TO RIGHT: WILLIAM CROWDER, RALPH ZUNDEL, JOEL PONDER, CHARLSIE PONDER, ALFRED LEWIS, UNIDENTIFIED, AND HAROLD KECH. BACK ROW: WILLIAM BISGROVE, LAWRENCE NUNNS, EDWARD WORRELL, C. ADAM KRESS, JOHN TUMBLIN, BAXTER WHITTEN, AND WILLIAM HOLMES.

THE SEMINARY'S DINING HALL WAS A FAMILY GATHERING PLACE. PRESIDENT AUSTEN KENNEDY DE BLOIS IS SEATED AT THE FAR RIGHT OF THE FRONT TABLE, WITH HIS RIGHT-HAND-MAN, DR. HARRY WATSON BARRAS, SEATED, WHERE ELSE, AT THE PRESIDENT'S RIGHT. AT THE OTHER END OF THE TABLE FACING THE CAMERA IS PROFESSOR JOHN B. CHAMPION.

took an additional $20,000 to renovate the building so that it could house the library and music rooms in addition to serving as student housing.

In 1927 the Seminary rented a house on Eighteenth Street at $375 a month for student housing and classrooms. In 1928, the Seminary bought its fourth building, 1810 Rittenhouse Square, a four-story building for student housing. It contained eighteen separate rooms and housed a new Dining Hall. The first meal was served there at 6:00 p.m. on Monday, September 17, 1928. The following year, students began operating the Dining Hall and were able to eliminate the operating deficit, which for the first two years had averaged some $6,000 annually. The purpose of the Dining Hall went far beyond the utilitarian purpose of feeding people. It was a gathering place for spiritual rejuvenation, social fellowship, and relaxation. Within a year, walls were cut and doors built to join this building with the Seminary's two others on the Square.

In 1930, the school purchased the buildings at 1808 and 1816 Rittenhouse Square at a total cost of $255,000. In 1931, it added 1818

A VIEW OF THREE OF THE SEMINARY'S BUILDINGS FROM THE PARK ON RITTENHOUSE SQUARE.

Rittenhouse Square for $80,000, thus increasing its frontage on the beautiful Square to 126 feet.

These purchases were enabled in part by another anonymous gift announced by Dr. Maxwell in 1930, this one coming in the form of an irrevocable trust worth $500,000. This gift also contributed to a 12.5 percent raise in faculty salaries.

The Seminary's net assets had grown steadily from the beginning. It started with nothing in February of 1925. Within a month it had $26. By the close of the first year, the Seminary could claim $1,308,058 in assets. By May of 1929, the figure had risen to $2,711,712. After ten years, the Seminary's assets totaled $3,343,690.

In 1927, the Seminary received a $3,000 gift, the interest of which was used to establish the Seminary's first scholarship fund for needy students. Several additional scholarship funds were begun during the de Blois years, during which the Seminary established a relationship with the University of Pennsylvania's Graduate School resulting in five full scholarships being awarded each year to Eastern Seminary students who were also interested in graduate work in another field. A couple of decades later, Stanley Nodder, Jr., the Seminary's current chairman of the Board, would take advantage of this opportunity.

MEMBERS OF THE 1930 GRADUATING CLASS. IN THE ORIGINAL PHOTO, ONE COULD SEE THE LEGS (FROM THE KNEES DOWN) OF THE WOMAN IN FRONT. BUT SOMEONE IN THOSE EARLY DAYS, ERRING ON THE SIDE OF MODESTY, COLORED IN THE LEGS NOT ONLY ON THIS PHOTO, BUT ON THE PHOTOS OF OTHER GRADUATING CLASSES AS WELL, THUS TEACHING WOMEN NEVER TO SIT IN FRONT.

AN INDUSTRIOUS COMMUNITY

The activities being undertaken by faculty and students during the de Blois years portray a close community bustling with energy. The president's secretary, Rose E. Rowe, through interviews and questionnaires, gathered accounts of students' life histories and ministry activities. By 1935, she'd filled five bulky volumes.

In addition to their administrative and teaching responsibilities, several faculty members found time to write. Faculty made contributions to the book *The Evangelical Faith*. Edited by Dr. de Blois, it addressed the basic principles of the gospel. Dr. Gorham authored *The Status of Weekday Church Schools in the United States*, while Dr. Champion wrote four books: *More Than Atonement*, *Why Modernism Must Fail*, *Sovereignty and Grace*, and *Personality and the Trinity*.

Faculty also contributed to *The Christian Review*, a quarterly theological journal published by the Seminary and edited by the president. The inaugural issue came out in January of 1932.

A Glee Club of twenty young men was formed in the fall of 1927 and performed at first in local churches and eventually up and down the Eastern seaboard. Among the other student organizations were the Missionary Volunteers, the Evangelistic Association, the League of Evangelical Students, the Homiletic Society, and the Athletic Association.

Beginning in the early 1930s, students, under the supervision of a faculty committee and under the auspices of the Evangelical Association, were required to engage in some sort of Christian service outside the classroom. This requirement made the Seminary unusual if not unique among theological institutions.

Dr. Livingston was the driving force behind it. In a typical month during the 1933–34 school year, the Eastern Seminary student body collectively preached 376 sermons, delivered 48 addresses, taught 387 Sunday School lessons and 108 City Mission classes, conducted 88 prayer meetings and led 74 youth meetings, rendered 396 musical services, visited hospitals 99 times, oversaw 78 professions of faith, 88 reconsecrations and 7 baptisms, did 14 radio talks, and distributed 259 gospels and 1,730 tracts.

In 1930, a group of students was inspired by a talk given by their president, and wanted a vehicle through which to become more articulate in the expression of their faith. Out of this initiative a Debating Society was born.

The holistic concerns of the Seminary's leadership extended even to the area of physical fitness. Wrote Dr. de Blois, "The care of the body is very apt to be neglected in institutions which specialize in the things of the soul. By reputation, at least, if not in reality, theologues are apt to be anemic and somewhat frail." Thus, during the 1930–31 school year the Seminary embarked on a program of physical fitness for students, arranged by Board member Charles R. Towson in cooperation with the Philadelphia chapter of the YMCA. Both male and female students participated in regular programs of physical fitness.

The Seminary's leadership maintained a strong concern for students' welfare. As a result of a rash of illnesses in 1929, an infirmary, staffed by a registered nurse, was established in 1930. Also in the early 1930s, the Seminary responded to the problem of loneliness commonly experienced by the wives of Seminary students, especially those not accustomed to city life. The Hypatia Club, essentially a women's fellowship group, was established and led by Mrs. Donald Gorham. In 1934, Miss Irene Jones was hired as dean of women.

In the summer of 1930, the Seminary developed a detailed list of rules and regulations regarding student discipline, resulting in widespread and emphatic protests, even from some of the most respected students. The outcome was the formation of a Student Governing Board, which succeeded at addressing disciplinary concerns while providing students with a sense of autonomy.

A LEADING VOICE

Dr. de Blois wrote in *The Making of Ministers*, "It is probably true, as a prominent educator has recently said, that no theological institution in the United States has ever grown with such rapidity into such a position of acknowledged strength and remarkable competency as The Eastern Baptist Theological Seminary in Philadelphia."

Indeed a conference held in March of 1931 illustrated that the young seminary was becoming a leading voice in the broader church community. At the suggestion of Dr. Laws, the presidents of conservative theological seminaries were invited to come to Philadelphia to discuss their common interests. Among those in attendance were representatives from Kansas City Theological Seminary, Northern Theological Seminary, Westminster Theological Seminary, the National Bible Institute, and the Gordon College of Theology and Missions. The conference illustrated also that the Seminary, while devoted to its Baptist denomination, was not narrowly Baptist in orientation.

Throughout his tenure, Dr. de Blois spent a considerable amount of time on the road, promoting the Seminary. He was surprised to learn that other seminaries had established regular programs of visitation at undergraduate institutions for the purpose of student recruitment. Though loathe to compete against other schools, he was always glad to answer questions about Eastern.

In his annual report to the Board in 1930, President de Blois stated that during the year he had written some three thousand letters and conducted about eighteen hundred interviews and conferences with students, teachers, and others. He also delivered forty-four outside addresses, including at Wheaton (Illinois) College, Broaddus College in West Virginia, and Denison University in Ohio. He apologized for what he considered to be a low number of outside appearances: "I feel that I have possibly been somewhat remiss."

THE STUDENT COUNCIL IN 1932. THIRD FROM THE LEFT IN THE BACK ROW IS CULBERT G. RUTENBER IN HIS STUDENT DAYS AT THE SEMINARY. FOURTH FROM THE LEFT IS FUTURE INTERIM PRESIDENT HENRY OSGOOD. ELDON KOCH IS AT LEFT IN FRONT AND AT RIGHT IS WALTER KALLENBACH, WHO WAS BLIND.

Toward the end of his tenure as president, Dr. de Blois began receiving many speaking invitations from churches and State Conventions on the West Coast, where during the 1933–34 academic year he spent nearly three weeks.

Even with all this, the president found time to write five books during his tenure as president: *Some Problems of the Modern Minister*; *John Bunyan, The Man*; *Fighters for Freedom*; *Evangelism in the New Age*; and *The Church of Today—and Tomorrow*. All his books enjoyed a healthy circulation both in the United States and in Canada.

But during the 1934–35 academic year, it became evident that both the years and the relentless pace were taking their toll on the president,

BY TODAY'S STANDARDS IN THE CLASSROOM, THE SEATS WERE HARD, THE LIGHTS WERE DIM, THE DESKS WERE SMALL, AND THERE WAS NO AIR CONDITIONING AND NO PLACE TO PLUG IN A LAPTOP.

A MUSIC STUDIO AT THE SEMINARY'S FIRST CAMPUS. MUSIC WAS A HIGH PRIORITY IN THE EARLY YEARS.

now in his early sixties. Two years previously Dr. de Blois had lost his wife, and it could be said that he never fully recovered from that loss.

In a note written from London in the early 1930s to Professor Barras, Dr. de Blois made reference to his weak heart: "I suppose this heart of mine will get me sooner or later—I hope it is later." In *The Making of Ministers*, Dr. de Blois made reference to a "three months' hospital experience in New York City" during the 1934–35 year.

As a result of his recuperation period, Dr. de Blois "regained much of his old-time power," in the words of Professor Barras, who wrote a concluding chapter in *The Making of Ministers*. But Barras added that "such gain can be maintained only by a less strenuous life."

THE SEMINARY'S INSIGNIA WAS USED ON THE CATALOG FOR THE FIRST TIME IN 1927. NEITHER THE SEMINAR PUBLICATIONS NOR THE BOARD MINUTES PROVIDE SPECIFIC DETAILS OF ITS ORIGIN. THE GREEK READS, "THE WHOLE GOSPEL FOR THE WHOLE WORLD." GREEK SCHOLARS, HOWEVER, CAN RECOGNIZE A FEW TECHNICAL ERRORS IN ITS FORMULATION.

Dr. de Blois's announcement that he would retire as of the end of the school year in 1936 was met with the deep regret of virtually everyone associated with the Seminary community, though he would continue as editor of *The Christian Review*. Wrote Barras:

"We shall follow our beloved friend and leader with our affection and our prayers, feeling grateful to God for the privilege of having these years of sweet fellowship on the pathway of life. May these later years become richer, more serene and more glorious until the Master says, 'It is enough, come up higher.'"

Ironically it was Dr. Barras who was the first (in 1937) to go "up higher." And on August 9, 1945, Austen Kennedy de Blois, having accomplished his mission of transforming an infant seminary into a vital, leading force in the arena of higher theological education, passed away.

President Austen Kennedy de Blois poses with the faculty in the early 1930s. Front row, left to right: Professors Arthur Harris and Barnard Taylor, Dr. de Blois, and Professors John Champion and James Maxwell. Included in the back row are Professors Carl Morgan, Harry Barras, Wilber Elmore, David Jamison, Donald Gorham, and L. Sarle Brown. The last two are unidentified.

The Seminary Under Gordon Palmer

Filling the void left by the departure of Dr. de Blois would be a tall order indeed. The Seminary had looked northward for its second president. For its third, it would look westward, all the way to California. Dr. Gordon Palmer was serving happily and successfully as the minister of First Baptist Church, Pomona. According to Gordon H. Baker in *What God Hath Wrought*, Dr. Palmer had no thoughts of moving anywhere, let alone to a new seminary some three thousand miles away to become its president. Thus, he was somewhat surprised when trustees asked him to consider their offer.

Stating that he wanted to be open to the guidance of the Holy Spirit, Dr. Palmer committed the matter to prayer. Eventually, he wrote a letter to the Seminary's Board in which he stated that if trustees and faculty were unanimous in favor of his coming, he would consider the offer a call from God. Apparently such unanimity was reached, as a call was given to Dr. Palmer on May 12 of 1936. The new president arrived in Philadelphia in December of that year.

In many ways, the odds were stacked against Dr. Palmer. In the early years the country remained in the throes of the deepest economic depression in its history. Providing education at very little cost became more difficult during the mid-1940s, as enrollment increased sharply, as it would during the Vietnam War era two decades later. (History has shown that war has a positive effect on Seminary enrollment.)

During his administration, Dr. Palmer had to provide leadership in a wide variety of areas, including continually revising and perfecting the curriculum, replacing key faculty, addressing accreditation issues, expanding the physical campus in order to accommodate the Seminary's growth, and determining how the

Seminary should address the theological controversies that had been building within the denomination.

LEAVING THE CITY

During the de Blois administration, there had been talk about moving the location of the Eastern Seminary campus. There would be similar talk in the 1990s about moving to St. Davids to join Eastern College. Nevertheless, Gordon Palmer to date remains the only president in the Seminary's history to oversee a campus relocation.

Toward the end of the 1920s, a discussion among Board members and loyal friends of the school had taken place regarding the best location for the Seminary. President de Blois characterized the opposing viewpoints as follows: "Many people felt that a theological seminary should be situated in some sweet saints' rest of a suburban or rural locality, where the noises and conflicts of the great city would not disturb the meditations of pious theological students. Others argued that a modern minister should

also be a real man, that he should live in the midst of things, and that he should touch elbows with the crowd."

A committee consisting of President de Blois, Professor Maxwell, Curtis Lee Laws, Gordon Baker, and Ralph Levering was formed to look into the matter. The president visited theological institutions in Chicago, New York, Boston, and elsewhere. The committee discovered that schools located in suburban or rural areas were trying to find ways to get to the city. It concluded that Eastern Seminary "should be located in the heart of a city, where it can come into intimate contact with the life of the metropolis and the activities of its churches."

No doubt, there was uneasiness among some—given the Seminary's commitment to be involved with the world—about moving away from the city. But the Seminary in the late 1930s faced the very practical problem of having outgrown its seven-building campus. The first option was to erect another building at the same location. This option was denied due to zoning laws. The trustees made an offer to purchase the Penn Athletic Club in order to remain in the city, but it was not accepted, and the Seminary could not afford to go higher.

When the opportunity came along in 1939 to purchase the Green Hill Farms Hotel, located at the edge of the city at the intersection of Lancaster and City Avenues, the trustees decided to jump. At $650,000,

PRESIDENTS AUSTEN KENNEDY DE BLOIS (LEFT) AND GORDON PALMER WERE BOTH ASSISTED BY SECRETARY ROSE E. ROWE, A NATIVE OF ENGLAND.

the luxury hotel, which came with a swimming pool and a beautiful sunken garden and was located near the Overbrook Golf Club, was considered a bargain. Some believe the price was driven down because of a highly publicized murder committed in the underground passageway between the hotel and the maids' quarters a few years earlier. (As far as is known, there have been no murders on the property since!)

Dismay over leaving the city is evident in the 1941–42 catalog, which states that trustees approved the move to Overbrook "with great reluctance." For several years afterward, the yearly catalog stated that the Seminary was "of the city, but not in it."

The actual move was accomplished in February of 1940. One of the first orders of business was to remove all the liquor stored in the hotel's basement until it was ready for the hotel bar. The bar, incidentally, was located just off the dining room in what is now the Presidents Room at the Seminary. Thus it could be accurately observed that the portraits of the Seminary's top leaders through the years have been hanging in a bar!

The Seminary's new facility provided rooms for all single students and gave the Seminary much-needed space to expand. Late in 1945, the Seminary purchased the Wynnewood Apartments, one block away, for $210,000 to house married students with children. The following year it purchased (for $102,000) the Lancaster Apartments on Lancaster Avenue primarily to provide suitable accommodations for professors.

Richard Shearer, a 1943 alumnus of the Seminary, recalls that the move had little effect on the strong sense of community at the Seminary: "It was a happy place. We did everything together. We would sing while we cleaned the dishes." What changed, however, was the nature of the field work. Instead of witnessing on city streets, more and more students were doing ministry in such venues as suburban hospitals.

FACULTY CHANGES

With the deaths of Professor Wilber T. Elmore in 1935, and Drs. Harry Watson Barras and Barnard C. Taylor in 1937, the Seminary lost three charter professors who had played key roles during its formative years. Among the professors who resigned for various reasons during the Palmer era were charter professors David Lee Jamison and John B. Champion, as well as Drs. Benjamin T. Livingston and Donald R. Gorham.

One of the many indications of the Seminary's growing prestige was the resignation of yet another charter professor, Dr. William W. Adams, who left Eastern Seminary in 1946 to become president of Central Baptist Theological Seminary in Kansas City. Dr. Carl Morgan succeeded him as professor of New Testament Interpretation and Greek. Thus, of the fourteen faculty members Dr. Palmer "inherited" in 1936, only five remained when his presidential tenure ended in 1948.

Dr. Palmer took the matter of selecting new faculty with utmost seriousness. He stated in one his reports to the Board, "I believe men should be called to teach at Eastern just as surely as men are called to be pastors."

Some of those who emerged to fill these posts were destined to take their place among the most deeply loved and widely influential professors in the Seminary's history.

Professor W. Everett Griffiths, a Theology instructor since 1930, succeeded Dr. Taylor as professor of Old Testament Interpretation and Hebrew. Harold Blatt remembers being stretched under Dr. Griffiths toward new ways of understanding the Old Testament: "He encouraged us to be open-minded. He changed our minds without changing our faith."

Professor Culbert G. Rutenber in 1941 succeeded Dr. Jamison as the chair of the Philosophy of Religion. Cubby had begun as a professor at

the Seminary two years earlier. By most accounts, he was the most popular professor in the Seminary's history, capable of taking the driest topic imaginable and bringing it to life. Dr. Rutenber eschewed the traditional lecture style. He never used notes, and was not averse to leaning on his desk or even standing on it occasionally.

Dr. Rutenber is remembered by many for his sense of humor. One year, Miss America, an outspoken Christian, came to the Philadelphia area to speak to youth. The Seminary was in some way associated with the event. Harvey Bartle, the longtime Board treasurer, commented on how bad Professor Rutenber looked compared to the attractive young woman. Cubby seized the moment by responding, "I may not be the most handsome man around, but I'd put my face up against Miss America's anytime."

And yet he was very serious about the stands he took for justice. As an unabashed pacifist, he stood virtually alone in the national scholarly circles in which he walked, and yet was accepted and admired because of his intelligence, his charisma, and his respect for others. Dr. Rutenber was a social activist long before it was popular to be one, and as such became something of a gadfly within the Seminary community as he pressed the administration toward more progressive policies with regard to its treatment of African Americans, who at one time were not permitted to live on campus or to use the Seminary's swimming pool.

Rutenber recalls taking African American student Ernie Johnson by the hand in the late 1940s and accompanying him into the Seminary's segregated swimming pool. All the other white people left. But within a few minutes, one of the female students decided to go back in. She was joined by others. A seed had been planted.

To many of his students Dr. Rutenber was a role model. Says Tom McDaniel, "Cubby Rutenber was my hero. He helped me to understand that I was a racist, and, more than any person, awakened me to issues of justice."

In 1944, Professor Robert G. Torbet, who had spent several years as an instructor in the Collegiate Division, took over as chair of Church History. Though he sometimes came across as being quite formal in the classroom, many remember Dr. Torbet as being sociable and congenial outside of class. He was active in organizing student meetings and also in counseling students. A consummate scholar, Dr. Torbet's 1950 book *A History of the Baptists* became a classic text for a whole generation of Baptist scholars. Amazingly, it remains in print fifty years after it was written.

Professor Albert G. Williams began at the Seminary in 1943 as professor of Evangelism and director of Placement and Practical Work, replacing Dr. Livingston. Two professors hired during the Palmer years came from Northern Baptist Theological Seminary in Chicago. Dr. William E. Powers succeeded Dr. John B. Champion in 1941 as chair of Theology. Gordon Baker described Powers as a man of "unusual ability," adding, "Students who entered his classroom soon knew they were with a master in his field."

Dr. C. Adrian Heaton arrived from Northern in 1946 to become the head of the School of Christian Education. For the next thirteen years, he and his wife, Ada Beth, built this department into one of the finest in the country. Ada Beth Heaton was the first female professor in the Seminary's history.

PROFESSOR CUBBY RUTENBER KNEW HOW TO MAKE STUDENTS LAUGH, BUT HE ALSO KNEW HOW TO MAKE THEM THINK, PARTICULARLY IN THE AREA OF SOCIAL JUSTICE.

In 1938, the Seminary's first librarian, Eleanor Price, resigned. Her assistant, Josephine Carson, took over. Though the Seminary's first two librarians were women, there would not be another female in that position until the 1990s. William J. Hand, an instructor in the Science Department of the Collegiate Division, became librarian in 1946. Dr. Hand left that post in 1970, but would return later in his career for interim periods of service even into the 1990s.

STAYING TRUE TO THE DENOMINATION

During the 1940s the Seminary and Dr. Palmer resisted the pressure that was being applied from some quarters to leave the denomination over theological issues. Two major splinter groups left the Northern Baptist Convention (NBC) in the 1940s: The General Association of Regular Baptists and the Conservative Baptist Association. One professor, Clarence Roddy, and a dozen or so students left the Seminary for the newly created Denver Conservative Baptist Seminary. But as an institution, the Seminary remained true to the commitments of its founders by attempting to be a leavening influence, instead of withdrawing.

SEMINARY PROFESSORS AND INSTRUCTORS IN THE 1940S: FRONT ROW, LEFT TO RIGHT: ARTHUR HARRIS, WILLIAM POWERS, CARL MORGAN, PRESIDENT GORDON PALMER, CUBBY RUTENBER, ROBERT TORBET, AND ALBERT WILLIAMS. MIDDLE ROW: EVAN REIFF, JAMES H. TELFORD, L. SARLE BROWN, HELEN ANDERSON, WILLIAM HAND, AND W. EVERETT GRIFFITHS. BACK ROW: ALEXANDER GRIGOLIA, CLARENCE S. RODDY, SAMUEL ORTEGON, AND JOSEPH R. BOWMAN.

THIS AD APPEARED IN A 1948 ISSUE OF *THE WATCHMAN-EXAMINER*, THE FLAGSHIP PUBLICATION OF THE FUNDAMENTALIST MOVEMENT IN ITS EARLY YEARS.

In its early years, the denomination looked askance on the Seminary. In the years since 1950, which is the year the National Baptist Convention became the American Baptist Convention (in 1972, the name changed again to American Baptist Churches USA), relations between the Seminary and the denomination would grow warmer. Through the years, several Seminary alumni and faculty, as well as one of its future presidents (Lester Harnish) would serve one-year terms as ABC president. Two of the Seminary's future presidents—Daniel Weiss and Robert Campbell—would serve as the denomination's top executive, Campbell before and Weiss after his tenure at Eastern Seminary.

Dr. Palmer's presidency was characterized by the strong desire to serve students, faculty, and staff. He led the effort to develop a retirement plan for faculty and staff. And early in his tenure, he oversaw the development of a six-year program in which students could earn both the Bachelor of Arts and the Bachelor of Divinity degrees at the Seminary. In 1938, the State Board of Education in Pennsylvania approved this program, but the American Association of Theological Schools was not so certain.

FINANCIAL PRESSURES

It could be argued that for one brief moment in the spring of 1925, the Seminary's leadership had no concerns about financial support. Since then, all the Seminary's presidents have had to concern themselves with questions surrounding from whence the money would come to support an institution seeking growth in one form or another. The financial challenges during the Palmer era were exacerbated by the economic depression and World War II. In one five-week period in 1941, the Seminary's investments plummeted in value over $150,000.

Among the cost-cutting measures taken by Dr. Palmer was to cease publication of *The Christian Review*, a ten-year-old periodical edited by Dr. de Blois that contained scholarly essays as well as news from the Seminary. The president regretted taking this action, but cited the periodical's low circulation and the high cost of publication. In its place, the Seminary began publishing *The Easterner*.

President Palmer oversaw the development of scholarship funds to help students for whom financial circumstances presented an obstacle to seminary education. In fact, he donated all his honoraria to this cause.

The Seminary's financial concerns were no doubt heightened by the April 1943 death of Ralph I. Levering, who had served as chair of the

Finance Committee from the founding of the Seminary. Mr. Levering in 1934 took a major cut in salary when he left his position with the West Philadelphia Title and Trust Company to become treasurer at Eastern Seminary.

Ralph Levering was the first in a long line of men and women who have served the Seminary through the years by virtue of their financial knowledge and business acumen. Wrote Gordon Baker in *What God Hath Wrought*, "Few people will ever know what Mr. Levering meant to Eastern. It was through his sane advice that the large gifts received by the Seminary in those early days were wisely invested, and the financial interests of Eastern safely guarded."

Among those who have donated similar skills and talents to the Seminary through the years have been Board presidents Charles Walton, Jr., Paul Almquist, Frank Middleswart, Maurice Workman, and Stanley Nodder, Jr., as well as trustees David Montgomery, Ralph Wolfe, and Nola Falcone.

In September of 1943 the Seminary hired Rev. P. Vanis Slawter on an ad hoc basis as a "field representative," the modern-day equivalent of a development officer. And in associa-

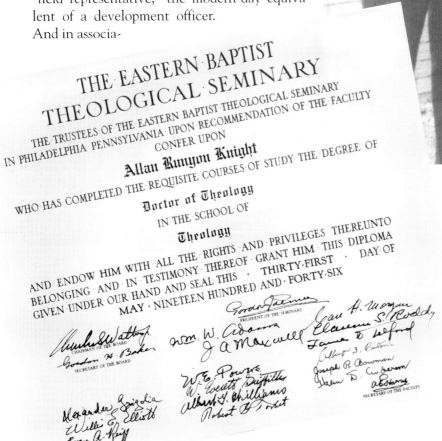

As far as it can be determined, Dr. R. Allan Knight (Th.D. '46) and Jeanette (Knight) Dube ('35) are the oldest living brother-and-sister tandem to have graduated from the Seminary. Dr. Knight's diploma appears to the left.

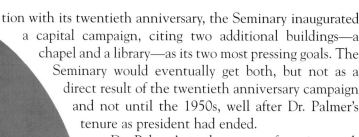

tion with its twentieth anniversary, the Seminary inaugurated a capital campaign, citing two additional buildings—a chapel and a library—as its two most pressing goals. The Seminary would eventually get both, but not as a direct result of the twentieth anniversary campaign and not until the 1950s, well after Dr. Palmer's tenure as president had ended.

Dr. Palmer's twelve years of service mark the longest tenure of the Seminary's presidents to date. He resigned on March 16, 1948. Until its next president arrived in 1950, the leadership of the Seminary was placed in the hands of a Steering Committee, co-chaired by Dean Carl Morgan and Treasurer Harvey Bartle.

Upon Dr. Palmer's departure, the main building on the Seminary campus was named "Gordon Palmer Hall." Dr. Palmer spent twenty-eight years on the Board of Trustees. He made many appearances on campus until his death on November 15, 1976.

LEFT:
CHARTER BOARD MEMBER REV. P. VANIS SLAWTER SERVED THE SEMINARY AS A FIELD REPRESENTATIVE (DEVELOPMENT WORKER) IN THE 1940S. PHILLIPS STUDIO

RIGHT:
PAUL ALMQUIST'S (LEFT) MORE THAN FIFTY YEARS OF SERVICE TO EASTERN SEMINARY BEGAN WITH HIS PARTICIPATION IN THE TWENTIETH ANNIVERSARY CAPITAL CAMPAIGN. NATIONAL PHOTO SERVICE

"The Whole Gospel to the Whole World"

ANNIVERSARY CAMP...

HEAD

THE ANNIVERSARY CAMPAIGN
OF
THE EASTERN BAPTIST THEOLOGICAL SEMINARY

FIRST YEAR GOAL $335,000

To accomplish these (3) projects:

1. Erection of a <u>Memorial Chapel</u> $125,000
2.   "   "   <u>Classroom Building</u>   175,000
3. Expansion of the <u>Library</u>   35,000

TOTAL $335,000

A SEVEN POINT PROGRAM
IN ADDITION

4. Erection of an <u>Auditorium</u>   6. Endowment of Professional Chairs
$150,000 $100,000 ea.

5. Liquidation of <u>Dormitory Mortgage</u>   7. Establishment of Scholarship Fellow-
$150,000   ship Funds $5,000 ea.

This picture was taken in May of 1937 at Rittenhouse Square, after Dr. Gordon Palmer became president, but before the move to Overbrook was even a twinkle in his eye. Anderson Studios

RIGHT:
THIS PHOTO FEATURES THE CHAIRMAN OF THE BOARD AND THE PRESIDENT WHO HAVE GIVEN THE MOST YEARS OF SERVICE TO THE SEMINARY. CHARLES S. WALTON, JR., SERVED FOR TWENTY-ONE YEARS, AND GORDON PALMER FOR TWELVE. IT WAS TAKEN AT THE SEMINARY'S 1948 COMMENCEMENT.

BELOW:
A DINNER IN SUPPORT OF THE SEMINARY'S TWENTIETH ANNIVERSARY CAPITAL CAMPAIGN. NATIONAL PHOTO SERVICE

Posing outside the Overbrook Presbyterian Church
are President Gordon Palmer and several faculty
members including a hand-clasping Professor Arthur
Harris. On the far right is Adrian Heaton, who is
standing next to Robert Torbet. To the left of
President Palmer is W. Everett Griffiths.

WORD HAS IT THE CHORAL GROUPS LED BY ROBERT
BOWMAN SOUNDED EVEN BETTER THAN THEY LOOKED.

THIS ROOM, WHICH IN THE YEAR 2000 IS OCCUPIED BY
MOSES KUMAR, VICE-PRESIDENT FOR FINANCE AND
OPERATIONS, WAS ONCE A PLACE WHERE MEN AND
WOMEN GOT TOGETHER FOR A DATE.

When the Seminary moved to Overbrook, chapel was held in the veranda of the main building. This area is known today as the Koinonia Center.

THE TRADITION OF EAT-
ING TOGETHER FAMILY
STYLE REMAINED FOR
OVER TWO DECADES
AFTER THE SEMINARY
MOVED TO OVERBROOK.

TREASURER DR. HARVEY
BARTLE WAS PART OF THE
LEADERSHIP TEAM THAT
SERVED IN LIEU OF A
PRESIDENT BETWEEN THE
GORDON PALMER AND
GILBERT LEE GUFFIN
ADMINISTRATIONS.

THE SEMINARY'S SWIMMING POOL WAS
SEVENTY-FIVE FEET BY THIRTY FEET. IT
REMAINED OPEN UNTIL THE EARLY 1980s.

The Gilbert Guffin Years

chapter

I n January of 1950, Gilbert Lee Guffin began his duties as the Seminary's fourth president and the first of three alumni up till now to serve their alma mater as president, the others to follow being Lester Harnish and Robert Campbell. Dr. Guffin had graduated from Eastern Seminary in 1935 with a Bachelor of Divinity (B.D.) degree. He went on to earn Master of Theology (Th.M.) and Doctor of Theology (Th.D.) degrees from the Seminary. Having come to Philadelphia from "the sticks" (his words) of Alabama, his rich experience at the Seminary spawned a love with the city and with the Seminary's mission that would continue for many years after his presidency ended.

Dr. Guffin is the only president in the Seminary's history to have been chosen from the ranks of its Board of Directors, not including Interim President Henry Osgood in the 1970s. Guffin had been elected to the Board in 1941 while serving as pastor at First Baptist Church in Merchantville, New Jersey. After that, he served as pastor of First Baptist Church in Jasper, Alabama, but he was soon tapped by Howard College (now known as Samford University), and it was there where Dr. Guffin would establish his credentials for becoming a leader in the field of graduate theological education.

Dr. Guffin had become widely known for founding and directing Howard College's Extension Division for Christian Training. Known as the Howard Plan, it had spread throughout the South and even into some parts of the Northern United States.

GILBERT LEE GUFFIN RETURNED IN 1950 TO SERVE HIS ALMA MATER AS PRESIDENT.

Much in tune with the Seminary's founding values, President Guffin sought to infuse the Seminary's alumni with evangelistic fervor. In a 1958 newsletter column, for example, the president pointed out that Baptists in Pennsylvania were in decline, but that there were more Eastern alums (288) in Pennsylvania than there were Baptist pastors in other states.

He wrote, "There are enough Eastern alumni alone, if their evangelistic concern is deep enough and if they meet the necessary conditions, to turn the tide . . . Brethren, let us rise to the challenge of our responsibility not only in Pennsylvania, but elsewhere as well. May the Holy Spirit give us wisdom and enduement adequate for the needs we face."

A COLLEGE IS BORN

A soft-spoken, cultured and very spiritual leader, Dr. Guffin was a problem solver. It did not take him long after arriving at Eastern to erase the Seminary's $50,000 deficit. He also tackled the thorny problem of accreditation. As far as the Seminary's Board and administration were concerned, the plan of offering a continuous education from college on through seminary was working well. But the model was one that accreditation officials did not recognize. They were bothered, for example, by the lack of a clear distinction between faculty Seminary and Collegiate Division faculty.

Concerns over accreditation were registering a negative impact. Something clearly had to be done. Either the Seminary had to establish a college as a separate institution, complete with its own campus, or the Collegiate Division would have to be closed. In the early 1950s, the Seminary did not have the money to make the former choice. But trustees knew how important the Collegiate Division had been through the years. Making the latter choice would have meant cutting deeply into the core of the Seminary's founding mission.

The problem resolved itself when the Walton estate, eight miles away in St. Davids, Pennsylvania, was placed on the market. The estate, known as *Walmarthon*, consisted of forty-five acres of beautiful land, as well as several buildings in "move-in" condition. The Seminary was able to purchase the estate at the remarkably low price of $650,000. Suffice it to say that the fact that Charles S. Walton, Jr., was serving as chairman of the Board did not hamper the Seminary's ability to find a bargain!

Eastern Baptist College in St. Davids was incorporated on July 11, 1952. In addition to purchasing the college campus, the Seminary turned over one-fifth of its investment assets to the College as seed money for its endowment. Despite all this, according to President Guffin, the establishment of the College actually benefited the Seminary financially because the parent institution was relieved of the responsibility of paying

PROFESSOR ADRIAN HEATON MAKES A POINT WITH PRESIDENT GUFFIN, OR AT LEAST PRETENDS TO DO SO FOR THE CAMERA. IN THE BACKGROUND IS THE CHRISTIAN EDUCATION BUILDING, WHICH PREVIOUSLY SERVED AS THE CLUBHOUSE FOR THE OVERBROOK GOLF COURSE. THE BUILDING HAD FOUR BOWLING ALLEYS AND SOME HANDBALL COURTS IN THE BASEMENT. IT WAS RAZED IN THE 1960S AND REPLACED WITH THE SEMINARY'S WESTERNMOST PARKING LOT.

IN 1952, THE SEMINARY'S COLLEGIATE DIVISION WAS DISCONTINUED AND EASTERN BAPTIST COLLEGE WAS BORN WITH A BEAUTIFUL CAMPUS, THE FORMER WALTON ESTATE, *WALMARTHON*, IN ST. DAVIDS.

college faculty and staff. The Seminary's financial assistance to the College was given on the condition that should the College ever abandon the doctrinal basis on which it was begun, all the College's assets would revert to the Seminary. From 1952 to 1987, the Seminary and College would be led by a common president and Board of Directors.

As it had to some extent when the Seminary moved to Overbrook some twelve years earlier, so the tenor of the campus changed when eighty-seven young men and women moved from Overbrook to St. Davids. Harold Blatt was a student government leader in the early 1950s. He remembers regular meetings with Dean Carl Morgan, who asked the young Blatt to exercise more control over his fellow students. It seemed a week did not go by without a fire alarm going off, or the air being let out of someone's tires, or a car being hoisted onto blocks. That all changed when the Collegiate Division moved out. Contemporary pranksters at Eastern College should be glad to know they are upholding a longstanding tradition.

MRS. CURTIS LEE LAWS TOOK PART IN THE 1951 GROUND-
BREAKING CEREMONY FOR THE CHAPEL BUILDING THE
SEMINARY HAD LONG BEEN SEEKING.

THE CHAPEL BUILDING, SEEN HERE UNDER CONSTRUCTION, WAS
THE GIFT OF MARGUERITE TREAT DOANE IN MEMORY OF DR. LAWS
AND OF HER FATHER, WILLIAM HOWARD DOANE. LES WALLACE

THE PHOTO OF THE FINISHED CHAPEL WAS TAKEN NOT LONG
AFTER ITS COMPLETION IN SEPTEMBER OF 1951, AS EVIDENCED
BY THE LANDSCAPING THAT REMAINED TO BE DONE.

A NEW CHAPEL AND LIBRARY

The Seminary trustees in 1950 decided to purchase a house for use
by the president. It was located on Remington Avenue in Wynnewood,
about a mile from the campus. It was also during the Guffin administration that the Seminary would acquire the
new chapel and library buildings it had long
been seeking.

The chapel building came in the form of
a gift from Marguerite Treat Doane, a friend
of Susan Tyler Laws, the widow of Dr. Curtis
Lee Laws. Mrs. Laws, who had been serving
on the Board since her husband's death in
1946, brought Mrs. Doane with her to an
Executive Committee meeting of the Board
in 1950. At that meeting Mrs. Doane
expressed her desire to give to the Seminary
a new chapel building as a memorial to Dr.
Laws and to her father, William Howard
Doane, who in the late nineteenth and early
twentieth centuries had achieved some distinction as a hymn writer.

The 600-seat Curtis Lee Laws Memorial
Chapel, built and furnished at a cost of
$413,000, was dedicated in 1951. The lower
level of the building was dedicated as the
William Howard Doane Hall of Sacred
Music.

HAROLD BLATT (RIGHT), SHOWN HERE
WITH ALUMNUS FOSTER WILLIAMS, SO
IMPRESSED ADMINISTRATORS WITH HIS
FUND-RAISING ABILITIES AS A STUDENT IN
THE EARLY 1950S THAT THEY HIRED HIM
RIGHT OUT OF SCHOOL FOR THAT
PURPOSE AT $3,800 A YEAR. LES WALLACE

Doane Hall was equipped with a music library, as well as ten, sound-
proof practice rooms, in each of which was located either a piano or a
manual pipe organ. Seminary catalogs in the mid-1950s refer to a museum just off the foyer "containing original manuscripts of compositions by
Beethoven, Mozart, and others. . . ." Those manuscripts—or at least some
of them—would eventually find their way to a Seminary safe, where they
would remain for over four decades.

A successful thirtieth anniversary capital campaign enabled the Seminary to build a new library and classroom building at a cost of $260,000. The new structure, de Blois Hall, connected Gordon Palmer Hall with the old library and classroom structure. Ground was broken in May of 1957, the same year the Seminary's current librarian was born. It was dedicated in 1958. The familiar sign facing motorists traveling east on Lancaster Avenue was not added until 1960.

In addition to a new building, the library during the Guffin years was the beneficiary of an impressive 4,500-volume collection donated by Philadelphia business executive Russell H. MacBride, who in addition to his books furnished the Seminary with a beautiful browsing room.

FACULTY CHANGES

As was the case with Dr. Palmer, Dr. Guffin presided over the coming and going of several key faculty members. Dr. Walter Bruce Davis, a Seminary alumnus and former missionary to what was then East Pakistan, served as a guest teacher during the 1954–55 academic year. In March of 1955, he became a full professor of Missions. Dr. Davis would remain at the Seminary well into the 1970s, serving for much of that time as dean.

In the early 1950s, Dr. Nelson Baker came to Eastern from the faculty of California Baptist Theological Seminary to replace Dr. Clarence S. Roddy. In 1952, Professor Griffiths resigned in order to go into the pastorate, though he was to return to the Seminary some fourteen years later. In the intervening years, Dr. Edward R. Dalglish served as professor of Old Testament Interpretation and Hebrew.

THE GIFT OF
MARGUERITE TREAT DOANE

THE CHAPEL IS DEDICATED
IN MEMORY OF HER FRIEND.
CURTIS LEE LAWS, D.D., LL.D.
1868–1946
A NOTED PASTOR, DISTINGUISHED
EDITOR OF THE WATCHMAN-EXAMINER
AND A CHARTER TRUSTEE OF THE
EASTERN BAPTIST THEOLOGICAL SEMINARY

THE HALL OF SACRED MUSIC IS
DEDICATED IN LOVING MEMORY
OF HER FATHER
WILLIAM HOWARD DOANE, Mus.D.
1832 – 1915
A PROMINENT BAPTIST LAYMAN,
SUCCESSFUL BUSINESS MAN, INVENTOR
AND RENOWNED COMPOSER OF
CLASSICAL AND SACRED MUSIC.

In 1951, Dr. Torbet left to go to work for the denomination's Board of Education and Publication. He was replaced by the gifted scholar Norman H. Maring. Dr. Maring would go on to serve the Seminary in several capacities, including professor, registrar, and director of admissions, until his retirement in 1982.

Drs. Adrian and Ada Beth Heaton left in 1959, but not before enabling the Seminary's Christian Education program to achieve standing as one of the best in the nation. During the 1950s, many institutions sought to recruit the Heatons. They chose to remain until 1959, when Adrian accepted the call to become president at California Baptist Theological Seminary.

Highly esteemed preacher Norman W. Paullin, pastor of the Grace Baptist Temple in Philadelphia, began teaching Homiletics part time at the Seminary in 1951, and in 1954 became a full-time professor in the chair of Homiletics. Englishman Dr. Arthur B. Crabtree arrived in 1957 as professor of Theology. Dr. Crabtree was known not just for his theological acumen, but also for his magnetic preaching. His teaching style was distinctly European, and his expectations of his students were exceedingly high.

The final addition to the faculty under President Guffin was Dr. Thorwald W. Bender, who came from Northern Seminary in the summer of 1959 to teach Philosophy of Religion and Theology. Dr. Bender replaced Cubby Rutenber, who accepted an invitation to teach at Andover Newton.

NEW VENTURES BEGUN

In addition to faculty and building additions, the Guffin years witnessed the launching of two institutions that have been important to the Seminary ever since. In 1952, the Women's Auxiliary support organization was formed, and it grew to several hundred members before long.

Through the years, the organization has recalled fondly the 1954 luncheon at which Ruth Teasdale inaugurated the organization's Scholarship Fund with a "pintful of pennies" totaling $6. Since then the organization has contributed tens of thousands of dollars in scholarship aid to students at the College and Seminary.

In 1994, the organization made the decision to focus its efforts on the Seminary. At the same time, the organization dropped *Women* from its title, thus officially opening the organization to the other gender. More than any other entity, the Auxiliary represents the many persons who from the beginning have operated behind the scenes to support and strengthen the Seminary. In addition to scholarship aid, the Auxiliary has sponsored numerous campus renovation and beautification projects, and members have collectively given hundreds of hours of volunteer service to the Seminary each year.

The first of the Seminary's four standing lecture series was launched in 1956 by Laura Moyer Swartley. In addition to honoring her husband, Wilmer C. Swartley, the purpose of the lectureship is to bring to the Seminary community outstanding preachers as well as teachers of preachers. The inaugural Swartley lecturer was Duke K. McCall.

Other highlights of the Guffin presidency include a 1955 tour of Palestine, led by the president. In those days, a tour was a tour! It lasted fifty-six days, from July 6 through August 30. Also in 1955 the film *Waterwheel Turning* was produced. It was the first of several films or videos to be produced for promotional or fund-raising purposes.

Dr. Guffin's resignation in 1961 took effect on May 31 of that year. He immediately rejoined the Seminary's Board, remaining a trustee until his death on July 13, 1992.

NORMAN MARING SERVED THE SEMINARY IN VARIOUS CAPACITIES, INCLUDING HISTORY PROFESSOR, REGISTRAR, AND DIRECTOR OF ADMISSIONS.

Esther George has given more years of on-campus service than anyone in the Seminary's history. Beginning in 1949, she served as secretary to five presidents. These days, her office is located in the Seminary Archive Room.

Among the faculty members who arrived during the Guffin years were Nelson Baker, shown with his portrait, and Norman Paullin.

THE LONE WOMAN IN THIS 1952 PHOTO OF THE BOARD OF
DIRECTORS IS MRS. CURTIS LEE LAWS, WHO CAME ONTO
THE BOARD AFTER HER HUSBAND DIED IN 1946.

51-134A

AN INFORMAL GAME OF BASEBALL WAS PART OF COMMUNITY LIFE IN THE 1950S. BUT SOMETIMES THE COMPETITION WAS INTENSE AND ORGANIZED. THE SEMINARY HAD BASKETBALL TEAMS FOR BOTH MEN AND WOMEN AND A FOOTBALL TEAM THAT PLAYED OTHER SCHOOLS FROM THE 1930S INTO THE 1960S.

51-136A

STUDENTS FRED BOEHLKE (LEFT) AND VINCE DE GREGORIS, BOTH 1952 ALUMS, CONFER WITH PROFESSOR RUTENBER. BOEHLKE WENT ON TO TEACH AT EASTERN COLLEGE AND DE GREGORIS AT THE SEMINARY.

LEFT:
ADA BETH HEATON (SHOWN HERE TALKING WITH A STUDENT) AND HER HUSBAND, ADRIAN, CONSTITUTED THE FIRST OF THREE HUSBAND-AND-WIFE PROFESSORIAL TEAMS IN THE SEMINARY'S HISTORY.

BELOW:
THE MUSIC PROGRAM WAS DIMINISHED, BUT BY NO MEANS DESTROYED AFTER THE ESTABLISH-MENT OF THE COLLEGE. SHOWN HERE IS THE 1956 VERSION OF THE SEMINARY SINGERS.

TOP:
MARY FRICK WAS THE CAMPUS NURSE FROM 1949 TILL
1966, WHEN SHE WAS REPLACED BY MISS ELIZABETH
BROADBROOKS. DR. G. H. FERGUSON, JR.,
MADE HOUSE CALLS AT LEAST ONCE OR TWICE A WEEK.

BOTTOM:
IN THIS PHOTO CAN BE FOUND THE SHORTEST AND
TALLEST EASTERN SEMINARY PRESIDENTS. PRESIDENT
GILBERT LEE GUFFIN (THE SHORTEST) IS SPEAKING TO
A GROUP OF COLLEGE FACULTY THAT INCLUDES FUTURE
PRESIDENT ROBERT CAMPBELL, THE TALL MAN IN THE
BACK ON THE LEFT. STANDING TO THE LEFT OF THE
PRESIDENT IS LYLE BRISTOL, COLLEGE DEAN. SITTING
IN FRONT OF CAMPBELL IS GEORGE CLAGHORN, WHO
WOULD ONE DAY SERVE AS DEAN AT THE COLLEGE.

THE ENTERING CLASS IN SEPTEMBER 1957

LEFT TO RIGHT:

A SUMMER DAY CAMP FOR YOUNG PEOPLE AGES SIX
THROUGH FOURTEEN BEGAN IN 1952. IT STARTED AT
9:00 A.M. AND ENDED AT 3:30 IN THE AFTERNOON.

DEAN'S SECRETARY JEANNE LEROY SERVED THE
SEMINARY FOR MANY YEARS.

A HISTORICAL PAGEANT IN MARCH OF 1950 FEA-
TURED LAWRENCE LAWSON ('51) AS PAUL AND
KARL KARPA ('55) AS NATHAN THE SCRIBE.

JAMES MEEK ('59), RONALD SCHLOSSER ('59),
TONY CAMPOLO ('60), AND WILLIAM KEYES ('60)
POSED FOR THIS PICTURE IN THEIR SEMINARY DAYS
OR SHORTLY THEREAFTER.

ABOVE:
IN THE LATE 1950S, BUSINESSMAN RUSSELL MACBRIDE
GAVE THE SEMINARY OVER FOUR THOUSAND QUALITY
BOOKS AND A BEAUTIFUL BROWSING ROOM.

LEFT:
ONLY TWO OF THE SEMINARY'S CHARTER PROFESSORS
REMAINED UPON PRESIDENT GILBERT LEE GUFFIN'S
ARRIVAL: ARTHUR HARRIS (SECOND ROW, FAR LEFT) AND
L. SARLE BROWN (BACK ROW, SECOND FROM LEFT).
PICTURED IN FRONT, LEFT TO RIGHT: VIRGINIA SNYDER,
CARL MORGAN, PRESIDENT GUFFIN, AND RUTH TEASDALE
(DEAN OF WOMEN). MIDDLE ROW: HARRIS, ADRIAN
HEATON, WILLIAM POWERS, NORMAN MARING, SAMUEL
ORTEGON, AND ALEXANDER GRIGOLIA. BACK ROW: EVAN
REIFF, BROWN, ROBERT TORBET, CUBBY RUTENBER, AND
WILLIAM HAND.

LAURA MOYER SWARTLEY'S GENEROSITY GAVE TO THE SEMINARY THE SWARTLEY LECTURESHIP SERIES, INAUGURATED IN 1956.

MRS. JOHN A. HAINER WAS AMONG THE FIVE WOMEN WHO STARTED THE WOMEN'S AUXILIARY IN 1952.

The Seminary Under Thomas McDormand

D r. Gordon Baker, one of the Seminary's founders, pronounced the benediction at the installation ceremony for Eastern Seminary's fifth president, Canadian native Thomas Bruce McDormand, in the fall of 1961. Dr. McDormand had begun his duties on September 1. At the time of his calling to the Seminary, he was serving as executive vice-president at Acadia University in Canada, alma mater of the Seminary's second president, Austen K. de Blois.

With experience as a pastor and editor of church publications, Dr. McDormand had also served on the Executive Committee of the Baptist World Alliance (BWA). While president at the Seminary, he presented a paper titled "The Effect of Tyranny on Human Personality" at a BWA International Congress. It was the fifth such paper he had presented since 1950.

Just twelve days into his new position, the president and the Seminary received a visit from Billy Graham, who filled Laws Chapel on September 13. Because Dr. McDormand was still familiarizing himself with the Seminary, he left it to his secretary, Esther George, to review the program for the day with Dr. Graham.

According to Miss George, there was quite a contrast between Dr. McDormand and his predecessor. Whereas President Guffin was calm and soft-spoken, President McDormand was energetic and witty. At a groundbreaking ceremony at Eastern Baptist College early in his administration, a photographer asked Dr. McDormand to turn over another shovel of dirt for the camera. The president responded, "What do you want me to do? Dig the basement?"

ON SEPTEMBER 13, 1961, EVANGELIST BILLY GRAHAM DREW A CROWD TO LAWS CHAPEL. LES WALLACE

RIGHT: BILLY GRAHAM MET WITH PRESIDENT THOMAS BRUCE McDORMAND IN HIS OFFICE.

President and Mrs. McDormand loved to entertain, and frequently invited faculty to their Seminary-owned home. According to Glenn Koch, who was an instructor at the College throughout the McDormand years, the president was a friend of the faculty in part because he brought to the institution a more open stance theologically. Because Dr. McDormand was not, in Dr. Koch's words, a "traditional evangelical," faculty felt freer to express ideas that pressed against the boundaries of rigid conservatism.

CAPITAL IMPROVEMENTS

Almost every president in the Seminary's history has had a chance to oversee a capital campaign. Dr. McDormand was no exception. In 1962, the Challenge Program for Progress was inaugurated, with the goal of raising $675,000 for the Seminary and the College. Among the results of the campaign was the establishment of a coffee shop in Palmer Hall to replace the Canteen, which despite its location in the basement of Palmer had been a primary gathering place for many years. Eastern Baptist College experienced considerable growth during the McDormand years, adding some $1.5 million worth of buildings and equipment.

In 1965, the Seminary celebrated its fortieth anniversary. It was honored to have as the speaker at the anniversary banquet William W. Adams, the last surviving member of the Seminary's original faculty.

In those days, Seminary-sponsored Holy Land tours were very rare, but they were a tradition at Eastern Seminary. Dr. McDormand continued the tradition in 1966 by leading a 21-day tour.

The Seminary library bolstered its collections in 1966 when it received bound volumes of *The Watchman Examiner* dating to 1819. The Seminary in its early years had shared a close relationship with this publication, the flagship of thought-

PICTURED WITH THE POPULAR CRUSADE EVANGELIST BILLY GRAHAM ARE (LEFT TO RIGHT) PROFESSOR THORWALD BENDER, COLLEGE PROFESSOR ERNEST ACKLEY, STEVEN BABBAGE (GRAHAM OFFICIAL), GRAHAM, PRESIDENT THOMAS MCDORMAND, AND DEAN WALTER BRUCE DAVIS.
LES WALLACE

CHARTER PROFESSOR WILLIAM W. ADAMS SPOKE AT THE SEMINARY'S FORTIETH ANNIVERSARY BANQUET. RICHARD L. W. REUSS

PRESIDENT THOMAS McDORMAND
(FRONT) POSES WITH HIS FACULTY.
BEHIND HIM, LEFT TO RIGHT, ARE
NORMAN PAULLIN, GUSTAVE GABELMAN,
CYRIL GARRETT, NORMAN MARING,
GLENN KOCH, WALTER DAVIS, WILLIAM
HAND, NELSON BAKER, CARL MORGAN,
ALBERT WILLIAMS, EDWARD DALGLISH,
ARTHUR CRABTREE,
AND THORWALD BENDER.

ful theological conservatism that Drs. Laws and de Blois had once served
as co-editors.

In May of 1967, the seeds of the coming age of technology were
planted at the Seminary. They came in the form of a videotape recorder,
which had been donated to the Seminary by the Alumni Association. In
fact, the community held a special chapel service to celebrate the arrival
of its new "toy," the idea being that preaching skills could be greatly
improved through the process of self-observation.

The first person to be recorded with the new equipment was Manuel
Avila, a 1950 graduate of the Seminary and the president of the Alumni
Association. It was one of many times through the years that the
Reverend Avila would demonstrate his faithful support of his alma mater.

The faculty member who had the most vested interest in the new technology was William D. Thompson, who had come to the Seminary in 1962 as associate professor of Homiletics and Speech. Widely respected as a teacher and practitioner, Dr. Thompson through the years would play a leading role in exploring the contributions of technology. In 1980, he secured a grant from the Association of Theological Schools to study the effects of videotaping on the improvement of preaching skills. Dr. Thompson was widely published in professional journals. His writings included the books *A Listener's Guide to Preaching*, *Preaching Biblically*, and *Listening on Sunday for Sharing on Monday*.

In fact, several faculty members reached a large audience through the printed word in the 1960s, largely in the form of pamphlets known collectively as the "Keys" series. *Keys to Effective Personal Prayer* was written by Professor Nelson Baker; *Keys to Theology* by Professor Arthur Crabtree; *Keys to a Christian Conscience* by professor Thorwald Bender; *Keys to the New Testament* by Professor Carl Morgan; and *Keys to the Old Testament* by Professor W. Everett Griffiths.

Dr. Griffiths, who had taught at the Seminary from 1930 to 1952, returned in 1966 for a three-year engagement teaching Old Testament, culminating in his retirement. He replaced Professor Edward R. Dalglish, who moved on to Baylor University.

W. EVERETT GRIFFITHS, SHOWN HERE WITH HIS WIFE, RETURNED TO THE SEMINARY IN 1966 AFTER A FOURTEEN-YEAR HIATUS.
RICHARD L. W. REUSS

In 1965, Helga Bender Henry, the sister of Professor Thorwald Bender, came to the Seminary as an instructor in the Christian Education Department. Four years later, her husband, Carl F. H. Henry would arrive to teach Theology.

In 1966, Martha Leypoldt was hired as a professor of Christian Education, having come from a similar position at North American Baptist Seminary in Sioux Falls, South Dakota. She was the second female professor to serve Eastern Seminary, but the first to arrive without a husband who was also a professor.

Other notable developments during the McDormand years include the following:

• Charter Board member Thornley B. Wood passed away in November of 1966.

• In 1962, the 16 millimeter, twenty-minute color film *Decades of Decision*, featuring the Seminary and the College was produced by the DeFrenes Company of Philadelphia.

• In 1967, alumnus L. Doward McBain ('43) became the first American Baptist Convention president to have graduated from both Eastern Baptist College and Eastern Seminary.

• In 1967, the primary degree for ministry preparation changed from B.D. (Bachelor of Divinity) to the current M.Div. (Master of Divinity).

President McDormand had planned to serve the Seminary through 1968, when he would retire. But citing family circumstances back home in Canada, he stepped down as president as of the end of 1967. He remained active in Canadian Baptist Churches for several years following his departure from Eastern, and also returned to the Seminary many times, including in 1970 when he received an honorary doctorate, until his death on April 3, 1992.

TOP:
GUSTAVE A. "GUS" GABELMAN SERVED THE SEMINARY AS DIRECTOR OF PLACEMENT THROUGH THE MCDORMAND YEARS.

BOTTOM:
JOAN WOOTERS, DIRECTOR OF PLACEMENT, HAS BEEN AT THE SEMINARY FOR NEARLY FOUR DECADES, HAVING ARRIVED IN 1963. HERE SHE IS CONVERSING WITH STUDENT DAVID SPROUT.
TEE ADAMS PHOTO

STUDENTS IN THE 1960s LOVED A
QUIET LIBRARY ALMOST AS MUCH AS
THEY LOVED DARK-RIMMED GLASSES.
BUT NEITHER COULD COMPARE WITH A
COOL DRINK AT THE SNACK SHOP.

TOP:
IN NOVEMBER OF 1966,
GILBERT (LEFT) AND
JAMES BAKER PRESENTED A
PORTRAIT OF THEIR FATHER,
FOUNDING TRUSTEE GORDON
H. BAKER, WHO PASSED
AWAY IN 1963.

BOTTOM:
GORDON PALMER (RIGHT)
SMILES AS HIS PRESIDENTIAL
PORTRAIT IS UNVEILED BY
CARL MORGAN. OTHERS
SHOWN ARE (LEFT TO RIGHT)
DEAN WALTER BRUCE DAVIS,
BOARD CHAIRMAN PAUL
ALMQUIST, AND PRESIDENT
THOMAS MCDORMAND.
CHARLES F. SIBRE

BOARD CHAIRMAN PAUL ALMQUIST AND PRESIDENT THOMAS MCDORMAND UNVEIL A PORTRAIT OF FOUNDING TRUSTEE RALPH MAYBERRY. RICHARD L. W. REUSS

FRONT ROW, LEFT TO RIGHT:
CYRIL GARRETT, CARL MORGAN, PRESIDENT THOMAS MCDORMAND.
BACK ROW: THORWALD BENDER, UNIDENTIFIED, NORMAN MARING,
WILLIAM HAND, AND NELSON BAKER. JOHN GOODWIN

Bob Hamilton arrived in 1965 and quietly served the Communications Offices at the Seminary and College for over thirty years.

The Lester Harnish Years *chapter*

A student back in the Rittenhouse Square days, J. Lester Harnish graduated in 1938 when Gordon Palmer was president. He was the second alumnus of the Seminary to go on to serve as president.

As with all previous presidents to that point, he had experience as a pastor. At the time he accepted the call to come to Eastern, he was serving at First Baptist Church in Portland, Oregon.

As with institutions in general, often a leader is brought in to address a particular area of concern. Such was the case with Dr. Harnish. Though he lacked experience in educational administration, he brought with him solid credentials as a conservative evangelical and highly effective pastor.

He was active, for example, in some of the trademark organizations of the conservative evangelical movement, including Youth for Christ and the Billy Graham Crusade. In fact he played a major role in organizing Graham's Portland Crusade in May of 1968.

Old Testament professor W. Everett Griffiths in the early 1950s had encountered some friction for teaching that some scholars believed there was more than one contributor to the book of Isaiah, even though Griffiths himself did not hold to this view. In any event, it is likely that some members of the Seminary's Board of Directors, and perhaps some friends of the institution as well, felt at the time that the Seminary was drifting too far from its conservative theological moorings. Lester Harnish was brought in to "right the ship."

THE EVANGELIST PRESIDENT

This assessment is certainly suggested by Dr. Harnish's stated goals as president, namely "to call the Seminary to renewed dedication to Jesus Christ" and "to a clear evangelical and conservative theological identification." And yet Dr. Harnish was not so conservative as to be unwelcome in the denomination, which as a whole has never been as conservative as the Seminary. In 1964, he had been elected to serve as president of the American Baptist Convention (ABC).

President Harnish began his duties at Eastern Seminary on January 1, 1968. It is the only time in the Seminary's history (not including acting or interim presidents) where there was not a single day between presidential administrations.

Through his time at the Seminary, the president lived out his conservative beliefs and emphases, particularly in the area of evangelism. The seminary newsletter, for example, records that Dr. Harnish in 1968

ABOVE:
SEMINARY ALUMNUS J. LESTER HARNISH, SHOWN HERE WITH HIS SECRETARY, ESTHER GEORGE, TOOK FOUR YEARS AWAY FROM HIS FIRST LOVE OF PASTORAL MINISTRY IN ORDER TO SERVE HIS ALMA MATER AS PRESIDENT.

LEFT:
THE FACULTY EARLY IN THE HARNISH ADMINISTRATION. FRONT ROW: W. EVERETT GRIFFITHS, WALTER DAVIS, PRESIDENT J. LESTER HARNISH, CARL MORGAN, AND ALBERT WILLIAMS. MIDDLE ROW: GUSTAVE GABELMAN, THORWALD BENDER, MARTHA LEYPOLDT, ARTHUR CRABTREE, AND NORMAN PAULLIN. BACK ROW: WILLIAM THOMPSON, NELSON BAKER, NORMAN MARING, WILLIAM HAND, AND GILBERT ENGLERTH. LES WALLACE

PRESIDENT J. LESTER HARNISH WITH
BOARD CHAIRMAN FRANK MIDDLESWART
AND HAROLD OCKENGA (RIGHT), WHO
SPOKE AT THE 1970 COMMENCEMENT.

led evangelistic meetings in West Virginia resulting in thirty decisions for Christ.

In May of 1969, President Harnish represented the Seminary at Billy Graham's New York City Crusade. That same year, the Seminary hosted an Evangelism Emphasis Day featuring black evangelist Tom Skinner. In 1972, the Seminary sponsored an evangelism conference and signed on as an official partner in a nationwide evangelistic effort "Key '73," scheduled for the following year.

The president's conservative influence was felt also in the speakers who came to the Seminary during his tenure. In 1970, for example, the commencement speaker was Harold Ockenga, widely regarded as an architect of the contemporary evangelical movement that began in the 1940s. The baccalaureate speaker that same year was Harold Lindsell, a strong proponent of biblical inerrancy and the longtime editor of *Christianity Today* magazine, which had been started in the 1940s as a conservative response to *The Christian Century*.

CONCERN FOR THE "DISADVANTAGED"

Lester Harnish's presidency was clearly influenced in part by the significant developments taking place in the country, including the Civil Rights movement and widespread rebellion against the social and cultural mores of the previous generation. For the first time in the Seminary's history, significant questions concerning injustices to African American people both within and outside the Seminary began to arise.

The record indicates that President Harnish made an effort to address these concerns. Prophetic voices calling for justice were welcome at the Seminary. Among them was Rev. Leon Sullivan, pastor of Zion Baptist Church in Philadelphia, who spoke at the 1968 baccalaureate.

Rev. Sullivan would go on to lead U.S. corporations in the 1980s to use their influence to end apartheid in South Africa.

The Seminary community in 1968 held a special chapel to assess, in the president's words, "the meaning of Dr. King's life, ministry, and death to America and to the cause of Christ in the country."

The roots of the Seminary's current emphasis on urban ministries can be traced to an inner-city mission course taught in 1969 by Rev. B. W. Johnson of the American Sunday School Union and Rev. Tom Ritter. At the time, Dr. Ritter was associated with Opportunities Industrialization Centers, begun by Rev. Leon Sullivan. He went on to join the Seminary's Board of Directors in 1969 and remains on the Board today.

Recognizing the need for many perspectives on issues related to race and justice, the president early in his administration established the President's Advisory Commission on the Disadvantaged. The commission's twenty members included trustees, students, and black pastors, as well as representatives from the Seminary faculty and administration.

Among the commission's goals was to find ways to bring more African American students to the Seminary. Despite the noblest of intentions, the success of this effort was limited. The term *disadvantaged* was never well-defined and was considered by some to be paternalistic if not slightly derogatory. Accounts of the commission's activities contained in the Seminary newsletter suggest that appeals for financial support for bringing minority students to the Seminary went largely unheeded.

A CHANGE IN BOARD PHILOSOPHY

In May of 1970 the Seminary's Governing Board took the historic step of providing for a limited number of non-Baptist "evangelicals of other denominations" to serve as directors. In accordance with the plan,

as many as nine of the thirty-six Board members could be non-Baptists. Only the twenty-seven Baptists, however, would retain the designation of "trustees." This opened the door for Dr. C. Everett Koop, chief surgeon at the Children's Hospital of Philadelphia, to become (in 1971) the Seminary's first non-Baptist Board member.

Dr. Harnish also presided over significant changes in the composition of the Seminary's faculty. Tragedy struck the Seminary early in the Harnish administration with the passing of the well-liked Professor Norman W. Paullin in 1968. In the summer of 1971, popular Christian Education professor Martha Leypoldt underwent brain surgery to remove a cyst that had paralyzed her right side.

At no time previously in the Seminary's history had a professor who was also an alumnus of the Seminary ever retired. But in 1969, three alumni, all of whom had to some extent become "institutions" at the Seminary, retired together: Professors W. Everett Griffiths and Carl H. Morgan, both of whom graduated in 1929, and Professor Albert G. Williams, who had graduated in 1930.

Two of those brought on to replace the men retiring were themselves destined to become institutions at Eastern Seminary. As were the professors they were replacing, both Thomas F. McDaniel and Glenn A. Koch were graduates of the Seminary, McDaniel in 1955 and Koch the following year. Dr. McDaniel replaced his former teacher Dr. Griffiths as professor of Old Testament and Hebrew, while Professor Koch, who had served as an instructor in Greek and Hebrew since the early 1960s, replaced his teacher and mentor Dr. Morgan as professor of New Testament and Greek. Both would remain with the Seminary for over thirty years.

In 1969, Dr. Carl F. H. Henry, joined the Seminary faculty as visiting professor of Theology, a position he held for about four years. The founding editor of *Christianity Today*, Dr. Henry is considered by some conservatives to be one of the greatest theologians in the history of the church. Perhaps more

Top to Bottom:
C. Everett Koop (right), the Seminary's first non-Baptist Board member, talks things over with Theology professor Carl F. H. Henry. Les Wallace

Fresh from the mission field in Japan, Thomas McDaniel took over in 1969 for his Old Testament teacher in his Seminary days, W. Everett Griffiths. Richard L. W. Reuss

Friends and colleagues W. Everett Griffiths, Carl Morgan, and Albert G. Williams retired together in 1969.

than at any other time in its history, faculty members in core disciplines, though respectful toward one another, were at odds over the expression of their theological beliefs. Both Professors Koch and McDaniel, early in their teaching careers, were called before the dean, president, and Board members to explain their positions. Dr. McDaniel over the next decade or so would have to do so on more than one occasion. But in all cases it was determined that his viewpoints, though quite different from Dr. Henry's, were nevertheless compatible with the Seminary's longstanding doctrinal basis.

Faculty additions during the Harnish years included (in 1970) Douglas Miller as professor of Christian Social Ethics. Professor Miller would remain with the Seminary for twenty years. In 1971, George Vanderlip replaced the popular Nelson B. Baker as professor of English Bible.

In 1970, Frank Veninga was named executive vice president at the Seminary, taking on many of the day-to-day operational responsibilities. Dr. Veninga's contribution to the Seminary during the 1970s is highly

regarded. Among his most important contributions was the character reference that contributed to the 1978 hiring of Manfred Brauch as vice-president and dean. Dr. Brauch's career at the Seminary would include a decade of service as president.

In 1972, Ruth McFarland, by virtue of her becoming the Seminary's registrar, became the first female administrator in the Seminary's history. She remains in that post today. A native of Australia, Ms. McFarland in 1970 had been hired away from a secretarial position with the United Nations. Through the years, she has represented a special sensitivity to the needs and concerns of minority and international students.

In 1972, Professor Leypoldt made a heroic effort to return to her teaching duties. After her brain surgery the previous year, she spent several weeks in a coma and had to undergo extensive therapy. Sadly, she did not have the physical strength to remain a teacher for long. She retired in 1973 and passed away in July of 1975.

FUND RAISING

President Harnish aggressively supported the Seminary's Expansion (capital) Campaign, launched in 1970 with the goal of raising some $2.1 million to benefit both the Seminary and Eastern Baptist College. Dr. Harnish traditionally began his newsletter columns with "Dear Friends of Eastern Everywhere" and closed them with "Yours and His." Not the least bit shy about asking for financial support, he dedicated many of his columns to supporting the campaign. Dr. Harnish also did his part by selling the Seminary-owned President's house and purchasing one of his own.

The Expansion Campaign succeeded in raising money for a scholarship in honor of the recently deceased Dr. Paullin and to help endow the establishment of the Thornley B. Wood Chair in Missiology. Thornley B. Wood, a businessman, was a charter member of the Seminary's Board.

The campaign also resulted in major improvements to Palmer Hall. A bookstore was built in the veranda that would remain until 1997. Also, Palmer was furnished with thirty-two apartments, twenty-nine dormitory rooms, some guestrooms and faculty apartments, an infirmary suite, three student kitchens, and a new elevator.

By this time, the trend toward off-campus living had begun and the days of the Dining Club were over. In 1969, the Seminary sold Baker Hall, which had been purchased as a place for married students with children to live. The building was largely empty, and now there was more room at Palmer. The building had been named in honor of Gordon Baker, whose name belongs on the small list of people who exercised profound influence on the Seminary in its early years.

In March of 1972, President Harnish announced his resignation, effective July 31. Noting his desire to return to his first love, he accepted the call to become senior minister at Third Baptist Church in St. Louis.

In May of 1972, at the last commencement under President Harnish, the Seminary awarded sixty-seven Master's degrees. It was the Seminary's largest graduating class since the 1940s. Dr. Harnish joined the Board in 1985, and continues as an emeritus member today at the age of eighty-six.

CLOCKWISE FROM TOP LEFT:
PRESIDENT HARNISH MET PRESIDENT
NIXON IN THE EXECUTIVE WING OF
THE WHITE HOUSE IN THE EARLY
1970S. HARNISH WAS IN TOWN FOR
THE ANNUAL MEETING OF THE NORTH
AMERICAN BAPTIST FELLOWSHIP.

WALLACE CHARLES "WALLY" SMITH
WAS A STUDENT DURING THE
HARNISH YEARS. HE WENT ON TO
BECOME THE SEMINARY'S FIRST
AFRICAN AMERICAN PROFESSOR,
AND SERVES ON THE BOARD TODAY.

JOHN ODURO, FROM GHANA, WAS
RESPONSIBLE FOR THE U.S. FLAG
BEING MOVED TO THE TOP OF A FLAG
POLE. IT HAD BEEN DRAPED OVER
THE ENTRANCE TO THE CHAPEL
BUILDING, BUT HE FELT IT WAS
UNFAIR FOR NON-AMERICAN STU-
DENTS TO HAVE TO PASS UNDER IT
EACH DAY.

Top:
The president greets one of the Seminary's many distinguished alumni, L. Doward McBain. Les Wallace

Bottom:
At one of the commencements during his tenure, President J. Lester Harnish posed with former Presidents Gilbert Lee Guffin and Thomas Bruce McDormand. Les Wallace

At the front table in this picture of the Board in the Harnish years are, left to right, Charles Colman, Jr., President Harnish, Chairman Frank Middleswart, and J. Lee Westrate.

CLOCKWISE FROM UPPER LEFT:
PROFESSOR ALBERT WILLIAMS OPENS
GIFTS AT HIS RETIREMENT PARTY IN 1969,
AS MRS. HARNISH LOOKS ON.
RICHARD L. W. REUSS

THE GLORY DAYS WERE GONE BY THE
1970S, BUT THE GUYS STILL PLAYED SOME
HOOPS. NUMBER 40 IS JAMES DUNN
('74). IN THE BACK ROW ON THE FAR
LEFT IS PROFESSOR DOUGLAS MILLER.
STANDING NEXT TO HIM IS GRANT WARD
('72). NUMBER 5 IS DAVID HARADER,
NUMBER 35 IS DAVID SPENCE, AND
NUMBER 4 IS LENNY HARMAN.

ERCEL WEBB (SECOND FROM LEFT) MEETS
WITH AFRICAN AMERICAN PASTORS.

The Seminary Under Daniel Weiss

D r. Henry R. Osgood, a member of the Seminary's Board of Directors, served as interim president until April of 1973. He had graduated from Eastern Seminary in 1932 and had spent most of his ministry career since then (thirty years) as pastor of First Baptist Church in Hyattsville, Maryland. From all accounts, Dr. Osgood was a stabilizing and positive influence during his eight-plus months as interim. He attempted to build unity and harmony among the faculty.

On April 11, 1973, Dr. Daniel E. Weiss, at age thirty-five, became the youngest president ever to serve the Seminary, a distinction he still holds today. Dr. Weiss possessed virtually all the qualifications one would expect from a seminary president. He had experience both as a pastor and as a professor, having taught ministry at Gordon Divinity School. At the time of his calling to the Seminary, he was serving as vice-president for Institutional Advancement at Gordon, suggesting he also had experience in the area of fund raising.

Though evangelism was not as high on President Weiss's priority list as it was for his predecessor, it was by no means unimportant, as signified by his representing the Seminary in the summer of 1974 at the historic Lausanne (Switzerland) International Congress on World Evangelization. By and large, President Weiss was perceived as a decisive leader with balanced theological views and also as an effective fund raiser who understood faculty and their concerns. In addition, he took steps to promote increased sensitivity and progress in the area of race relations.

In 1974, William J. Shaw, pastor of White Rock Baptist Church, taught a course at the Seminary as a guest lecturer. Dr. Shaw, the Seminary's 1994 Mitchell lecturer, in 1999 was elected president of the National Baptist Convention USA, the nation's largest African American denomination.

The first African American professor in the Seminary's history, alumnus Wallace C. "Wally" Smith started in 1979 working in the Office of Alumni Affairs and in field education. In 1981, he was named associate professor of Pastoral Theology and Ministry.

It should be noted, however, that urgings were coming from various quarters within the Seminary community to make an effort to create a more diverse faculty. At the November 17, 1978 faculty meeting, for example, Professor William D. Thompson moved for the dean to convene two task forces, one to explore concerns related to the education of women and the other related to the education of African American students. Implicit in this recommendation was the goal of having an African American presence on the faculty.

The first faculty member to come in under President Weiss was Eugene Wright, who in 1973 became the first to hold the Ralph L. Mayberry Chair in Evangelism. Dr. Mayberry, in his mid-eighties, was present for the installation.

Many other impressive faculty members were hired by President Weiss, including the much-beloved and dearly remembered Dr. Culbert G. Rutenber, who returned in 1974 to close out his career. "Cubby" had spent his fifteen-year hiatus teaching at Andover-Newton and at American Baptist Seminary of the West. He returned to teach Philosophy of Religion at the Seminary until his retirement in 1979.

Another of the Seminary's most distinguished graduates returned in 1974 to teach at his alma mater: the widely known and gentle-spirited professor of theology Bernard L. "Bernie" Ramm. Since graduating from the Seminary in 1941, Dr. Ramm had gone on to write fourteen books en route to achieving international recognition as a leading theologian.

Also in 1974, Myron and Janet Chartier, both of whom held Ph.D.s, became the first husband-and-wife professorial team to serve the Seminary since Adrian and Ada Beth Heaton in the 1950s. Dr. Myron Chartier was brought in mainly to direct the Seminary's new Doctor of Ministry program, which had been launched with twenty-two students in 1973 with Professor Thompson serving as acting director. Dr. Janet Chartier replaced the retired Martha Leypoldt as professor of Christian Education.

In 1978, President Weiss took the unprecedented step of bringing to Eastern Seminary the first non-Baptist professor in its history: theologian

Ronald J. Sider. Dr. Sider, whose denominational affiliation at the time was Brethren in Christ, in essence held the same theological and social values Professor Rutenber had represented for over four decades.

Dr. Sider was among the authors of the 1973 Chicago Declaration, a call for evangelical Christians to place social justice and concern for the poor alongside evangelism as essential priorities. In 1972, he founded Evangelicals for Social Action, the organizational entity through which he has pursued his theological and social goals for nearly three decades. Dr. Sider's bestselling book, *Rich Christians in an Age of Hunger*, published in 1973, awakened the hearts and minds of thousands of believers to the church's obligations to the poor.

Understandably, Professor Sider felt very much at home at Eastern Seminary, given its longstanding emphasis on evangelism and social concern as equal priorities, as reflected by the Seminary's motto: The Whole

Gospel for the Whole World. In 1989 Sider brought the ESA offices to campus, and they have been there ever since.

It was also in 1978 that Vince deGregoris came to Eastern Seminary as professor of Pastoral Psychology. In luring Professor deGregoris away from Andover-Newton Theological Seminary, one of the president's arguments was that Vince owed it to the Seminary to return to his alma mater because, after all, it was at Eastern Seminary where he had met his wife, Charlotte.

And it was also in 1978 that a full-bearded Manfred T. Brauch came to the Seminary as vice-president, academic dean, and professor of New Testament Interpretation. A native of Germany who had moved to the United States at age fourteen, Dr. Brauch had since 1971 been teaching New Testament at Northern Baptist Theological Seminary outside Chicago. Of all the many key people who came to the Seminary during the Weiss years, none would have a greater impact on the Seminary's future course than Dr. Brauch.

Reflecting the Seminary's desire to serve the Hispanic community, highly respected missiologist Orlando Costas arrived in 1979 as the Thornley B. Wood Professor of

MANFRED BRAUCH, SHOWN HERE WITH ASSISTANT SANDY WALLER, CAME TO THE SEMINARY IN 1978 TO SERVE AS PROFESSOR AND DEAN.

IN HIS SECOND GO-ROUND, PROFESSOR CULBERT G. "CUBBY" RUTENBER PROVED THAT HE COULD STILL MAKE PEOPLE LAUGH, AS HE DOES HERE WITH FORMER PRESIDENT LESTER HARNISH (LEFT) AND FORMER BOARD CHAIRMAN PAUL ALMQUIST. LES WALLACE

PROFESSOR RUTENBER ALSO PROVED, AMONG OTHER THINGS THAT HE COULD COORDINATE AN OUTFIT. HERE IS MAKING A POINT AMONG COLLEAGUES (LEFT TO RIGHT) NORMAN MARING, WALTER DAVIS, DOUG MILLER, AND BERNARD RAMM.

Missiology and director of Hispanic Studies. Professor Costas left in 1984 to become dean at Andover-Newton, and he passed away in 1987. Although Hispanic students have attended through the years, the Seminary has for various reasons struggled to sustain efforts to serve the Hispanic community to the extent it desires.

The final two professors who came to the Seminary during the Weiss years constituted yet another husband-and-wife team. In 1980, Peter Schreck arrived as assistant professor of Pastoral Care and Counseling. His wife, Carol, came on as adjunct professor in Counseling. She would be promoted in 1998 to associate professor of Marriage and Family Counseling after completing her doctoral studies. For twenty years, the Schrecks have played major roles in the Seminary's Doctor of Ministry program in Ministry to Marriage and Family, which Peter served as acting director from 1993 to 1996. In addition to teaching, Carol serves the Seminary as coordinator of Student Counseling.

PETER AND CAROL SCHRECK, IN 1980, BECAME THE THIRD HUSBAND-AND-WIFE PROFESSORIAL TEAM IN THE SEMINARY'S HISTORY. THEY ARE THE ONLY SUCH TEAM TO SERVE THE SEMINARY TODAY.

TWO DOCTOR OF MINISTRY PROGRAMS

Two of the three Doctor of Ministry programs in the Seminary's history were born during the Weiss years. In 1970, the Association of Theological Schools had given the official go-ahead for member institutions to launch Doctor of Ministry programs. As was the case with most of the early programs, the one begun at the Seminary in 1973 was generic in nature. Its primary goal was to increase competence in general pastoral ministry skills. By the mid-1980s the program had run its course. Among the reasons for its demise were its residency requirements, which made it difficult for people from outside the area to attend.

The Seminary's Doctor of Ministry in Ministry to Marriage and Family was launched in 1980 thanks to a $250,000 grant from the J. Howard Pew Freedom Trust. In many ways, this program was ahead of its time, due in part to its pioneering emphasis on family systems theory. Dr. deGregoris, Dean Brauch, Professors William D. Thompson, Myron and Jan Chartier, and Vice President for Development Craig Hammon all had a part in its development.

Since 1980, several seminaries have begun marriage and family counseling–related programs, but Eastern Seminary's program remains distinctive. While marriage and family therapy is an important aspect of the program, its emphasis is on doing pastoral ministry that is proactive in addressing the needs of marriages and families in the church. Dr. Myron Chartier served as director of the program from its inception until 1985. Dr. deGregoris directed the program from 1985 till 1993.

Following the presidents who had gone before him, Dr. Weiss provided leadership in the area of fund raising during his tenure, including in the fiftieth anniversary Partnership in Faith campaign to raise $1.5 million for the College and Seminary. As a result, the Seminary was able to build a modern communications center and a preaching chapel in Doane Hall. The plan for equipping the communications center called in part for the production of teaching videos for use outside the Seminary, but it never fully materialized.

In the summer of 1981, President Weiss resigned unexpectedly. He went on to serve as executive vice president at Pace University in New York City from 1981 to 1983. From 1983 to 1988, he served as executive director of the denomination's Board of Educational Ministries. Since that time he has been serving as the American Baptist Church's general secretary, the denomination's top executive post.

PROFESSORS VINCE DEGREGORIS (LEFT) AND MYRON CHARTIER HELPED CHART THE COURSE FOR THE SEMINARY'S PACE-SETTING DOCTOR OF MINISTRY PROGRAM IN MINISTRY TO MARRIAGE AND FAMILY.

As part of a class on pastoral care, Frank Veninga taught students the mechanics of baptizing in the Laws Chapel baptistry. His model here is Irwin "Larry" Brand. Students used Larry a lot for baptism practice because he was a big guy, and they figured if they could dunk him and bring him back up, they could pass the test with anyone. Richard L. W. Reuss

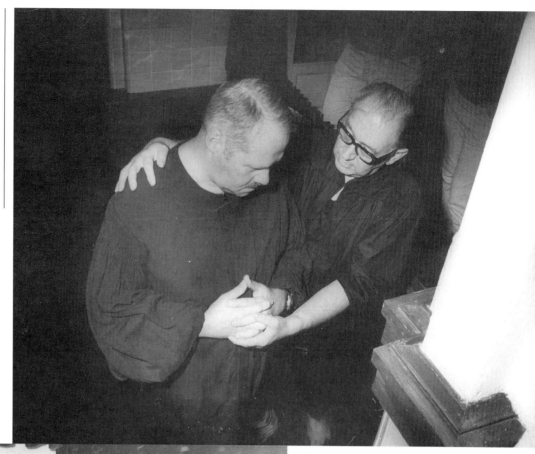

Supporting the staff's annual giving efforts are nurse Liz Marren, secretary Esther George, and library staffer David Koch.

BILL GRAY, PICTURED HERE WITH FRANK VENINGA, WAS AN ADJUNCT PROFES-
SOR AT THE SEMINARY IN THE 1970S. HE WENT ON TO SERVE AS A U.S. CON-
GRESSMAN, AND TODAY IS PRESIDENT OF THE UNITED NEGRO COLLEGE FUND.

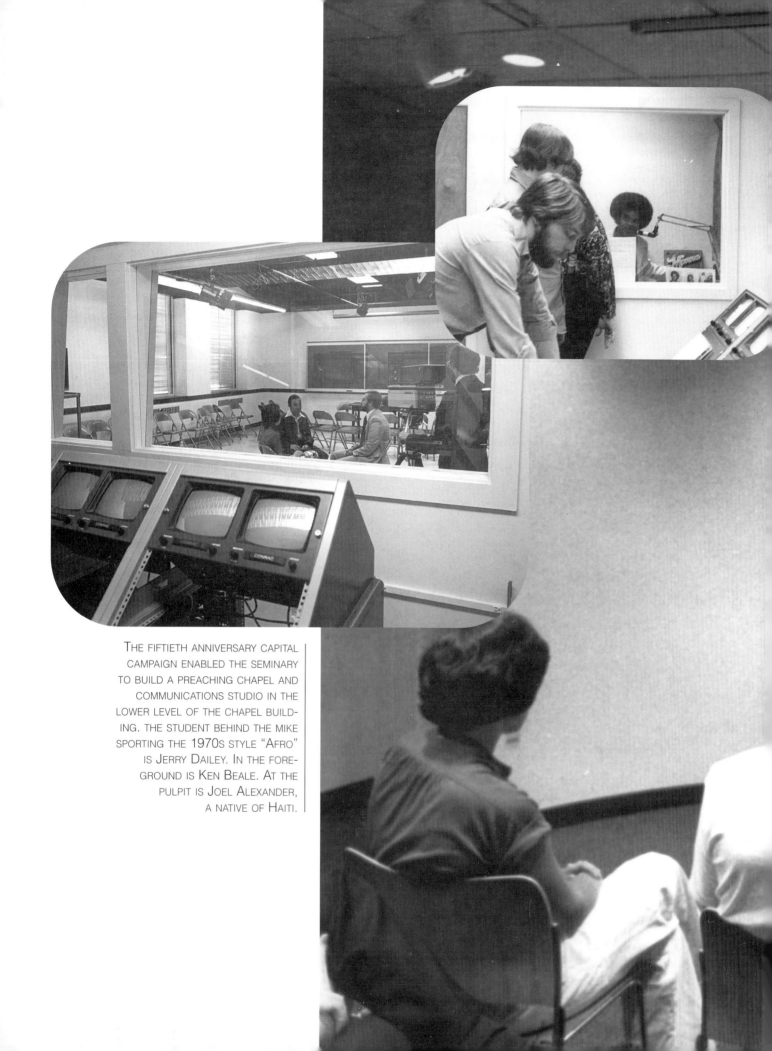

THE FIFTIETH ANNIVERSARY CAPITAL CAMPAIGN ENABLED THE SEMINARY TO BUILD A PREACHING CHAPEL AND COMMUNICATIONS STUDIO IN THE LOWER LEVEL OF THE CHAPEL BUILDING. THE STUDENT BEHIND THE MIKE SPORTING THE 1970S STYLE "AFRO" IS JERRY DAILEY. IN THE FOREGROUND IS KEN BEALE. AT THE PULPIT IS JOEL ALEXANDER, A NATIVE OF HAITI.

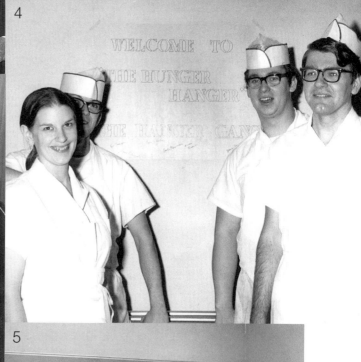

6

1. President Daniel E. Weiss is pictured here with 1950 alumnus Manuel Avila, Rolando Gutierrez from Mexico, and Board Chairman Frank Middleswart.

2. Professor George Vanderlip in the bookstore with students Ken Howard (left) and George Harkless.

3. A post-beard C. Everett Koop (center) with Board Chairman Middleswart and President Weiss.

4. The "Hunger Hangar" was the 1970s version of the Seminary snack shop. Third from the left is Ken Thompson, who gave it its name. His original sandwich, called the "Hangar," was made of pressed ham and grilled cheese on a Kaiser roll and is still remembered fondly by some at the Seminary. Richard L. W. Reuss

5. A class session in the Seminary's first Doctor of Ministry program. Richard L. W. Reuss

6. The 1974 graduating class.

Students prepare to depart for the annual seminarians' conference in Green Lake, Wisconsin. In front of the two columns is Professor Eugene Wright.

LEFT:
PROFESSOR BERNIE RAMM IS AMONG THE MOST DISTINGUISHED THEOLOGIANS TO HAVE GRADUATED FROM EASTERN SEMINARY.

RIGHT:
LIBRARIAN GILBERT ENGLERTH SERVED THE SEMINARY FROM 1970 TILL 1980.
PFAFF PHOTOGRAPHY

LEFT:
THE FACULTY EARLY IN THE WEISS YEARS. SEATED, LEFT TO RIGHT ARE WILLIAM THOMPSON, NORMAN MARING, PRESIDENT DANIEL WEISS, FRANK VENINGA, AND WALTER DAVIS. STANDING: GUS GABELMAN, GLENN KOCH, EUGENE WRIGHT, TOM MCDANIEL, DOUG MILLER, GEORGE VANDERLIP, GILBERT ENGLERTH, AND CARL HENRY.
PFAFF PHOTOGRAPHY

The Turbulent Decade of the 1980s

I n November of 1980, Ralph L. Mayberry, the last surviving member of the group of six ministers who founded Eastern Seminary on March 19, 1925, passed away at the age of ninety-two. Through the years, Dr. Mayberry had a long and faithful relationship with the Seminary, which he visited many times, including in 1940 when he received an honorary degree, in 1960 when he delivered the commencement address, and in 1973 when a chair was endowed in his honor.

A charter member of the Seminary's Board of Trustees, Dr. Mayberry served on the Board for fifty-five years until his death. For those familiar with his expressions of faith, he was a quintessential role model who in many ways represented Eastern Seminary's highest ideals. After serving Pennsylvania churches for twenty-five years, Dr. Mayberry moved to the West Coast to become executive secretary for the Los Angeles Baptist Mission Society. During his lengthy tenure there, forty-five churches were planted.

Ralph Mayberry was almost single-handedly responsible for a steady flow of students at Eastern Seminary who came all the way from the West Coast. Only in recent years did this stream begin to slow. In addition to spreading the gospel, Dr. Mayberry expressed his faith by taking a stand for justice, including by fighting the FBI during World War II over the unjust internment of Japanese-Americans.

Dr. Mayberry's passing was an inauspicious beginning to what was to become a very turbulent decade for Eastern Seminary. Never in its history had

the Seminary experienced more than two changes in presidential leadership in a given decade. Through the 1980s, there would be four such transitions, beginning with the resignation of President Daniel E. Weiss in 1981. Through the 1980s, the Seminary would experience the greatest financial crisis in its history, a crisis so severe that some insiders feared for the institution's very survival.

In the fall of 1982, the Seminary had set an enrollment record of 313, bolstered by 120 Doctor of Ministry students, many of whom were enrolled in the Marriage and Family program that had begun in 1980. But through the rest of the decade enrollment was stagnant, largely because of the continuing trend toward part-time, second-career students. It was in 1985 when the balance tipped for the Seminary, as for the first time in its history part-time students outnumbered full-time students. Fifty of the 71 new Master's students that year met the criteria for "second-career" status.

In 1985, the Seminary was still several years away from changing to a scheduling structure that accommodated part-timers. This made the effort to attract students extremely difficult for Admissions Director Steve Hutchison, a 1971 alumnus who came to the Seminary in 1984. Even though enrollment in 1987 reached 386, tuition income was under what had been budgeted because of the high percentage of part-time students. In part because of the trend toward specialized programs, the Seminary's original Doctor of Ministry program was discontinued in the mid-1980s.

THE ROBERT SEIPLE YEARS

Dean Manfred Brauch accepted the challenge to serve as acting president from 1981 until the arrival of Robert Seiple, who began his duties as the Seminary's eighth president in July of 1983. In some

ways, President Seiple, who had served as a marine navigator during the Vietnam War, did not fit the prototype for a seminary president. Unlike previous Eastern Seminary presidents, he had no formal theological education or pastoral experience. What's more, he was only the second president to have come to the Seminary from outside the ranks of the American Baptist denomination, as his roots were Conservative Baptist. (President McDormand was Canadian Baptist.)

The new president, however, was an energetic, visionary leader and an accomplished fund raiser, having served as vice-president for development at Brown University, in which role he had led a successful $158 million capital campaign. Such credentials were considered important, especially for the College, which was well into a fast forward expansion mode in terms of students, buildings, and programs.

In his inaugural address, President Seiple suggested what his primary mission would be as he spoke of the need "to create a critical mass of resources—people, ideas, programs, as well as dollars—that will allow dreams to transpire to the point of realization and implementation."

As evidenced by the participation of Prison Fellowship founder and president Charles Colson at his inauguration, President Seiple was well connected. Building on these connections, he sought to engage both the College and the Seminary in the moral, social, and political issues of the day. In 1984 he established the Evangelical Roundtable, which drew numerous religious and political leaders to Eastern schools for major annual conferences.

PRESIDENT SEIPLE MEETS ON THE STEPS OF LAWS CHAPEL WITH PROFESSORS MYRON (LEFT) AND JANET CHARTIER, AND WALLY SMITH.

U.S. Ambassador to the United Nations Jeane Kirkpatrick and economist Michael Novak participated in the inaugural Roundtable on the topic of "Christianity in Latin America." Other titles of Roundtable forums were "Christianity and the Arab-Israeli Conflict" (1985); "Evangelicalism: Surviving its Success" (1986); and "The Sanctity of Life" (1987).

President Seiple is fondly remembered by Seminary staff as a humble and likable leader. He made it a point to visit staff members on a regular basis. Frequently he would sit and have coffee with individuals just to find out how they were doing and to keep track of their lives. Aware that there were those who had concerns about his untraditional background, President Seiple read voraciously in theological literature and became a

powerful, articulate promoter of the Seminary's wholistic evangelical commitments, as well as a leading voice in the discussion of issues in theological education.

One of Professor Tom McDaniel's fondest memories is of meeting President Seiple in the coffee shop not long after Seiple's tenure had begun. The president informed the Old Testament professor that his hero from Old Testament times was King David. Now anyone who has taken Professor McDaniel for a class knows that he considers King David to be overrated, to say the least. Professor McDaniel seized the opportunity to compare and contrast King David, who put a premium on personal power and glory, with the prophet Jeremiah, a voice for the powerless and disenfranchised. A few years later at his going away banquet, President Seiple would tell his audience that his new Old Testament hero was the prophet Jeremiah.

THE DECADE OF THE 1980s WAS A TOUGH ONE FOR THE SEMINARY. BUT ALUMNUS SYDNEY KANE ('43) WAS AMONG THOSE WHO KEPT THE FAITH. HERE HE DISPLAYS THE LICENSE PLATE THAT CONTAINS THE MESSAGE HE INTERNALIZED AS A STUDENT BACK IN THE EARLY 1940s. "GO YE" IS PART OF THE SEMINARY'S SEAL.

The former president's memories of his time at Eastern, however, are not exclusively fond, largely because of the financial problems that had begun to plague the institution. "Those were rough years," he recalls. "If more than one thing went wrong in a day, you could be out of business. At least that's the way it felt. And after a while, it began to have an affect on the vision."

In October of 1986, the Seminary and College kicked off the largest capital campaign to that point in their history: the Decisive Years campaign. The original campaign goal was $14.1 million, but it was adjusted upward to $24.1 million based on a multimillion-dollar challenge commitment from a major donor.

Although the campaign raised millions of dollars, it fell far short of its ambitious goal (especially the Seminary's portion), in part no doubt because President Seiple felt called to a new ministry less than a year into the campaign. In 1987, he received an offer to serve as president of the highly respected, California-based evangelical relief and development organization World Vision. Thus, his time as president at Eastern Seminary ended on June 30.

The decision to leave Eastern Seminary and College was one over which the president agonized. But in the end, and due in part to the new biblical hero he had discovered at the Seminary, he could not turn down the opportunity to give his time, energy, and talents to directly serving the world's poorest and most downtrodden people. After leaving, Seiple served for two years on the Seminary's Board of Directors. His leadership at World Vision was marked by a phenomenal expansion of its relief efforts around the globe. In 1998, he accepted a new challenge working

with the U.S. State Department as ambassador-at-large for religious freedom.

TWO INSTITUTIONS, TWO PRESIDENTS

Through the decade of the 1980s it became more and more evident that the idea of one person serving as president over two institutions was no longer tenable. What had begun as the Collegiate Division of the Seminary in 1932 by the mid-1980s had come to overshadow the institution that had given it birth. Enrollment at the College between 1983 and 1985 alone had increased nearly 40 percent. Eighty-seven students had made the transition from Overbrook to St. Davids in 1952. By 1985, enrollment at the College had increased to 958. By any measure—students, annual budget, programs, or physical plant—Eastern College had far outgrown its mother institution and was pressing to take wings of its own.

Though the general missions of the institutions were similar, the administrative dynamics, specific goals, and student and donor clientele had for several years been moving in their own, distinct directions. Upon leaving Eastern, President Seiple strongly recommended to the Board of

PRESIDENT ROBERT A. SEIPLE POSES WITH THREE OF HIS PREDECESSORS. LEFT TO RIGHT ARE PRESIDENTS J. LESTER HARNISH, SEIPLE, GILBERT LEE GUFFIN, AND DANIEL E. WEISS.

LEFT TO RIGHT:
IN SEPTEMBER OF 1987, ROBERT CAMPBELL BECAME PRESIDENT OF EASTERN SEMINARY, AND ROBERTA HESTENES BECAME PRESIDENT OF EASTERN COLLEGE, AS THE MOTHER AND DAUGHTER SCHOOLS SET OUT TO PURSUE THEIR OWN IDENTITIES.

JUAN SAMUEL ESCOBAR RANKS AMONG THE CHURCH'S LEADING MISSIOLOGISTS.

LEADING BLACK THEOLOGIAN J. DEOTIS ROBERTS ARRIVED IN 1984.

ELOUISE RENICH FRASER BECAME THE FIRST FEMALE PROFESSOR IN THE SEMINARY'S HISTORY TO TEACH SOMETHING OTHER THAN CHRISTIAN EDUCATION OR MUSIC.
JOHN BENDER PHOTOGRAPHY

Directors that each school have its own president and administrative team. The Board took his recommendation seriously.

Thus, on September 1, 1987, Roberta Hestenes became the first president to lead only Eastern College, and Robert Campbell became the ninth president of Eastern Seminary. In addition to having separate presidents, the two schools took on separate development and financial officers. A single communications office continued to serve both institutions until 1991 when this final staffing link between the two schools was severed.

The choice of Robert Campbell as Seminary president was likely influenced in part by concerns that had been raised in some quarters about the non-ABC background of his predecessor. Unlike President Seiple, Campbell was an insider, having received four degrees from Eastern Seminary, including a Bachelor of Divinity (B.D.) in 1947 and an honorary doctorate in 1974. He had taught Biblical Languages at the Seminary and Religion at the College, and he had served as dean at American Baptist Seminary of the West for fifteen years. He was also a denominational man, having served as general secretary of the American Baptist Churches USA from 1972 until the time of his coming to Eastern.

The new president inherited an institution in financial difficulty. In the four years prior to his taking over, the Seminary had experienced year-end deficits of $283,000, $308,000, $295,000, and $384,000. The Seminary's aging buildings were falling into disrepair. Based on the projected influx of funds from the Decisive Years campaign, the Seminary spent some $2 million on such projects as roofing and masonry repairs. But most of the money it was expecting never came.

Some maintenance projects were delayed in midstream, due to lack of funds, resulting in a campus that belied its original beauty. Some students were embarrassed to invite friends to visit the campus. Employees

who left for one reason or another were not replaced. Others were laid off. At one point, the maintenance staff was down to one, and having incurred a debt of some $1.5 million for maintenance and renovation projects, those who controlled the Seminary's purse strings correctly perceived that their hands were tied.

SOME BRIGHT SPOTS

The decade of the 1980s was by no means void of bright spots. Among them was the launching of the Eastern School of Christian Ministry (ESCM) in 1983 under the leadership of Orlando Costas. This certificate program, which in the closing years of the millennium increased dramatically in popularity under the directorship of professor Ian Scott, represented the latest incarnation of the instinct of the Seminary's founders to provide training for all people, regardless of their level of preparation.

Other positive developments during the 1980s included the hiring of three key faculty members, all of whom arrived during the Seiple era. Elouise Renich Fraser, with a Master of Theology from Fuller and a Ph.D. from Vanderbilt, was installed in 1984 as assistant professor of Systematic Theology, thus becoming the first female full-time professor in the Seminary's history to teach in an area other than Christian Education. During her time at the Seminary, Dr. Renich Fraser has earned a reputation for encouraging students to integrate their theological learning with their personal spiritual growth. Later in her career at the

"WHO'S WHO?" STUDENTS OF 1986 ARE ERNIE AND MARIAN MITCHELL IN FRONT; BARBARA (WINSLEY) STEVENS AND MARCIA BAILEY IN THE MIDDLE; AND KEN WEISS, JOANNE WEISS, AND PHINEAS MARR III IN THE BACK.

Seminary (in 1998) she added the role of associate dean to her responsibilities. She is the only woman in the Seminary's history to hold the title of dean.

Also installed in 1984 was Dr. J. Deotis Roberts as Distinguished Professor of Philosophical Theology. A highly respected theologian, Dr. Roberts had made his mark as the primary architect of a more moderate version of Black Theology in answer to the more radical Black Theology movement led by James Cone. He came to the Seminary from the Interdenominational Theological Center, which he had served as president.

In 1985, Peruvian native Juan Samuel Escobar came to the Seminary as the Thornley B. Wood Professor of Missiology. An internationally respected missions scholar, Dr. Escobar has for the last fifteen years represented an excitement for missions and evangelistic witness that hearkens back to the goals and emphases of the Seminary's founders.

THE CRISIS CONTINUES

Accomplished Baptist scholar William H. Brackney came to the Seminary in May of 1987 as executive vice-president and dean, replacing Dr. Brauch, who had stepped down in order to return to teaching. It was left largely to President Campbell and Dean Brackney to address the Seminary's mounting indebtedness.

They had several factors working against them in addition to the general seminary enrollment trends mentioned above. The Seminary was feeling the financial effects of separation with the College. Having its own president and administrative leadership team entailed significant increases in operating expenses. Given that most institutions depend on their governing boards for financial support, both the College and the Seminary were hampered by the inherent limitations of one Board serving two institutions.

The operating deficits continued in the late 1980s. In fact, they became a yearly reality, threatening the Seminary's ability to maintain its accreditation. In the fiscal year ending in 1988, the deficit was nearly $600,000. Through these deficit years, the Seminary met yearly operating expenses mainly by borrowing against its endowment, as opposed to taking out a bank loan. This gave it greater flexibility in repaying the money. It had the obvious effect, however, of decreasing the earning power of the Seminary's financial investments.

It is no wonder that for those who reflect on the late 1980s, the two most commonly used words are "downward spiral." Because maintenance work took place in fits and starts as money would allow, the campus was frequently unattractive, which had a negative effect on student and staff morale. Decisions on tenure and promotions had to be put on hold. Additions to faculty or staff were out of the question. All of these factors conspired to diminish the school's image not just to potential students, but to potential donors. There was talk of adding evening classes mainly for the purpose of increasing tuition income.

There was also consideration of selling the Seminary campus and moving to the Eastern College campus in St. Davids. A task force of Board members and representatives of both schools studied the possibility of a university model in which the Seminary would become the graduate theological school of a larger institution. For numerous reasons, it concluded that such a structure would not be in the best interests of the particular mission of each school.

The Board realized that while borrowing from the endowment might be necessary on occasion as a stopgap measure, to do so year after year was a formula for disaster. Yet the trend would continue throughout the decade.

At one point during the 1988–89 fiscal year, the deficit for the year was projected to be $677,000. Thus, in March of 1989, the Board sum-

EN ROUTE TO LAWS CHAPEL DEAN WILLIAM BRACKNEY TALKS THINGS OVER WITH HIS IMMEDIATE PREDECESSOR, MANFRED BRAUCH.

CLOCKWISE FROM TOP LEFT:
PRESIDENT CAMPBELL WITH FORMER PRESIDENTS HARNISH AND WEISS.
CAMPBELL HELD THE ABC DENOMINATIONS' TOP EXECUTIVE POSITION WHILE
WEISS WAS PRESIDENT AT THE SEMINARY. WEISS

PROFESSOR RENICH FRASER IS KNOWN FOR HER COMMITMENT TO INTEGRATING
THEOLOGY AND SPIRITUAL GROWTH.

PROFESSOR ESCOBAR USUALLY HAS A SMILE ON HIS FACE, SO HERE HE MUST BE
MAKING AN ESPECIALLY IMPORTANT POINT.

GARDNER C. TAYLOR (LEFT), DUBBED BY *TIME* MAGAZINE AS AMERICA'S DEAN
OF BLACK PREACHERS, WAS THE MITCHELL LECTURER IN 1986. HE SHARES A
WORD WITH PROFESSOR DEOTIS ROBERTS. TO THE RIGHT IS FRANK MITCHELL.

moned trustee Paul Almquist to take a more active role in the day-to-day management of the Seminary. Dr. Almquist had served the Seminary faithfully for over four decades, including for ten years during the 1960s as chairman of the Board. It was largely through his influence that many key Board members through the years were drawn to Eastern Seminary. He had participated in some way in all the Seminary's fund-raising campaigns dating back to the 1940s. In 1950 he had met in Atlantic City with Marguerite Treat Doane to help pave the way for her gift of a chapel building to the Seminary. In 1989, he was prepared to do more.

Due in large part to Dr. Almquist's influence and to two large legacies, the 1988–89 deficit was far less than anticipated. In May of 1989, Professor Manfred Brauch, for the second time in his career, accepted the Board's challenge to become acting president following President Campbell's retirement on June 30. At the same time Dr. Brauch assumed the role of acting dean when Dr. Brackney resigned to assume the principalship at McMaster Divinity College in Ontario, Canada. (Glenn Koch had served as associate dean/dean of students under Brackney from 1987 to 1989.)

Dr. Almquist had helped to minimize the crisis. Nevertheless, as the decade of the 1980s drew to a close, the very future of Eastern Baptist Theological Seminary was uncertain.

THE SEMINARY'S BOOKSTORE AS IT LOOKED IN THE 1980S.

The Brauch and Rodin Years:
Return to Prominence in the 1990s

O n March 19, 1990, Eastern Seminary reached the age of sixty-five. Sixteen days earlier, Manfred Theophil Brauch had been appointed by the Board as the Seminary's tenth president. Significant difficulties had to be overcome to ensure a viable future. Faculty, staff, and student morale were at an extremely low ebb. The Seminary continued to experience the practical ramifications of its separation from the College. This entailed the challenge of re-creating the Seminary's identity and sense of mission, not to mention an independent donor base.

Except for widespread confidence in Dr. Brauch's leadership, there were few signs of hope on the horizon, so few that some were even suggesting it was time for Eastern Seminary to celebrate sixty-five years of rich and meaningful history and then close its doors.

The world was changing as it always has, and so was the church. But according to current Seminary president R. Scott Rodin, his predecessor did not have the luxury of making any ambitious long-range plans: "This was a period of crisis management. Manfred was the captain of a severely leaking ship, and his first priority was to keep it afloat." Fortunately for those who have loved the Seminary through the years and who love it today, Dr. Brauch would not only keep the ship afloat, but restore it to health and point it in a new and positive direction.

There are those, including longtime Old Testament Professor Tom McDaniel, who believe that Dr. Brauch was so successful in part because he never aspired to be president. Thus, he was motivated primarily by a sense of mission and love for the school and for the principles for which it stood. After all, the Board had recruited him as president when he served as acting president

from 1981 to 1983, but he declined. In 1986, he relinquished his role as dean because he missed the classroom. At first he said no again to the permanent presidency after becoming acting president in 1989. However, confronted with a school in crisis, he eventually relented.

In articulating his vision for the Seminary, Dr. Brauch stated that his goal was for it to become a "more significant force for the renewal of the church and in the divine work of human transformation to which the church is called."

Early in his administration, Dr. Brauch oversaw the development of a new mission statement for the Seminary. This process resulted in the addition of three words to the Seminary's longstanding motto, modifying it to read: "The Whole Gospel for the Whole World Through Whole Persons." The addition of "Through Whole Persons" represented an emphasis on spiritual formation, beginning with efforts to guide students toward "an awareness of their own brokenness" and the need for a "disciplined devotional life."

Arguably, the president's most important qualification for leadership was his warm and generous personality. Those who remember Dr. Brauch in future years will no doubt remember him smiling. His German accent was the target of many a barb, from students and staff alike. He took it all in stride, and joined the laughter.

Perhaps because he came from the ranks of the Seminary faculty, President Brauch understood what was important to his once and future colleagues. At times in its past, the Seminary faculty had been characterized by factions and disharmony. Dr. Brauch recognized the importance of a faculty that functioned together in unity and harmony.

LAYING NEW FOUNDATIONS

With the help of organizational consultant and friend of the Seminary Harold Howard, the Seminary was able to develop a five-year plan for 1990–95. It called, among other things, for a new Master of Arts program in Theological Studies, aggressive efforts to rebuild the Seminary's financial foundations, and the advent of block-scheduling, designed to attract more second-career students by allowing them to take several courses on a single day during the week.

Among Dr. Brauch's most important early accomplishments was the rebuilding of the Seminary's leadership team. Canadian-born Eric H. Ohlmann came to the Seminary in 1990 as vice-president/academic dean and professor of Christian Heritage. He has proved to be a tireless and meticulous administrator in the process of leading the faculty and developing and overseeing the Seminary's academic programs and policies.

That same year, Jamaican-born Horace O. Russell accepted the invitation to become the Seminary's first dean of the Chapel as well as professor of Historical Theology. Dr. Russell quickly earned the community's respect as a source of knowledge, comfort, and wisdom.

Dr. Harold Blatt, an alumnus from the 1950s who had previously served the Seminary and College as vice-president for Advancement, returned. The Brauch-Blatt team, further strengthened by the efforts of alumnus Dr. Douglas Whittle as director of Alumni/ae and Church Relations, founded an aggressive program of fundraising and built strong relationships with the Seminary's constituencies of friends, alumni, churches, and denominations.

Moses Kumar, a native of India, came to the Seminary in 1990 as an accountant. In

TOP:
IN THE SPRING OF 1990, ALEXANDER "SASHA" YUTCHKOVSKI (SECOND FROM LEFT) CAME TO THE SEMINARY AS THE FIRST SOVIET GRADUATE-LEVEL MINISTRIES STUDIES STUDENT IN THE UNITED STATES. HE IS SHOWN HERE WITH PROFESSOR GLENN KOCH, PRESIDENT MANFRED BRAUCH, AND GEORGE BOLTNIEW ('61). WALTER HOLT

BOTTOM:
DEAN ERIC OHLMANN, LIKE TWO OF THE SEMINARY'S ELEVEN PRESIDENTS, IS A NATIVE OF CANADA. JERRY MILLEVOI

1996, he became vice-president for Finance and Operations. His keen financial management, rooted in a strong sense of mission, has played a key role in the restoration of fiscal health to the Seminary.

In 1991, the Seminary began a successful experiment in the Department of Homiletics, or Preaching. Instead of a full-time professor, it hired two half-time teachers: Nancy Lammers Gross and Gerald R. Thomas. This approach in large part constituted recognition of the high percentages of female and African American students at the Seminary.

In 1992, longtime professor and librarian William J. Hand, who had returned to the Seminary as interim librarian, turned the job over to Melody Mazuk, who became the third female librarian in the Seminary's history and the first since the 1940s. Ms. Mazuk has proved to be the perfect choice to lead the Seminary into the contemporary technological age. In 1999 her position as "Library Director" was complemented by her additional appointment as associate professor of Theological Bibliography.

Also in 1992, the Seminary hired its first full-time African American female professor, Dr. Leah Gaskin Fitchue, as associate professor of Urban Ministry and director of Black Church Studies and Relations. It was under Dr. Fitchue's enthusiastic and aggressive leadership that the Seminary would bring into being Dr. Brauch's dream of a second Doctor of Ministry program in the Renewal of the Church for Mission.

Upon the 1993 retirement of Harold Blatt, President Brauch brought in R. Scott Rodin (pronounced roh DIN) as vice-president for Advancement. Not only did Dr. Rodin hold a Ph.D. in Theology, he also brought with him highly developed ideas on the relationships between and among spirituality, obedience, and stewardship which can be found in his *Stewards in the Kingdom*, published by InterVarsity Press in 2000.

Dr. Rodin went immediately to work, leading efforts to enhance the Seminary's public image and to open up new avenues of financial sup-

LEFT TO RIGHT:
HORACE O. RUSSELL, A NATIVE JAMAICAN, FOR OVER TEN YEARS HAS OVERSEEN THE
SPIRITUAL LIFE OF THE SEMINARY COMMUNITY. HE IS PICTURED HERE WITH HAITIAN-
BORN KETLEY PIERRE, WHO IS NOW ON THE MISSION FIELD IN NICARAGUA.

MOSES KUMAR, FROM INDIA, HAS BEEN THE SEMINARY'S CHIEF FINANCIAL OFFICER
SINCE 1996.

LEAH GASKIN FITCHUE (LEFT) TAUGHT URBAN MINISTRY CLASSES IN THE 1990S,
JUST AS LONGTIME BOARD MEMBER TOM RITTER (RIGHT) HAD DONE IN THE 1960S.

MELODY MAZUK HAS LED THE SEMINARY'S 135,000-VOLUME LIBRARY INTO THE
TECHNOLOGICAL AGE. PAUL EMMA

port. He would later take the lead role in directing the 1996–99 Forward
in Faithfulness capital campaign, and even found time to serve as an
adjunct faculty member teaching Theology. These credentials would
eventually lead to Dr. Rodin's succeeding Dr. Brauch as president.

The final faculty addition under President Brauch was Dr. Will
Barnes, who was hired in 1995 as director of Field Education and who has
added to these responsibilities the directorship of the Seminary's twenty-
year-old Doctor of Ministry program in Ministry to Marriage and Family.

A PROPITIOUS BEGINNING

Four months into Dr. Brauch's presidency, the Seminary would
receive a major and totally unanticipated boost. Suffice it to say that in
July of 1990, the Seminary community's appreciation for the music of
classical composer Wolfgang Amadeus Mozart skyrocketed. Eastern
College employee Judy DiBona, looking for records she thought might be
found in a Seminary safe, discovered original manuscripts from classical

composers, including Haydn and Strauss, the most notable of which was Mozart's "Fantasia and Sonata for Piano in C Minor."

The newly discovered manuscripts had been collected by hymn writer William Howard Doane, who died in 1915, ten years before the founding of Eastern Seminary. They were donated to the Seminary by Doane's daughter, Marguerite Treat Doane. Through much of the 1950s the manuscripts, as well as a Beethoven original autograph, were on display in a museum in the foyer of the Doane Hall of Sacred Music, located in the lower level of the chapel building. At some point, probably in 1957, they were removed, literally, for safe-keeping. As with baseball cards of that era, nobody knew that an original Mozart would one day be considered a highly valued prize. (The whereabouts of the Beethoven manuscript remains unknown.)

Judy DiBona's discovery could not have come at a better time for the Seminary, given its precarious financial situation. President Brauch called the Mozart manuscript "a gift from the Lord." Four months later, the manuscripts were auctioned off by Sotheby's of London, resulting in a net gain for the Seminary of some $1.5 million. It is understandable that President Brauch would consider the discovery a gift from the Lord, given that the Seminary's debt on capital renovations made in the late 1980s was $1.5 million.

BUILDING INFRASTRUCTURES

While it helped plug a gap, the Mozart discovery was nowhere near enough to solve the Seminary's financial problems. That would take a lot of time, hard work, and many, many miles by plane and car. As Dr. de Blois had done in an earlier era, Dr. Brauch traveled across the nation, usually accompanied either by Director of Development Harold Blatt or Director of Alumni/ae and Church Relations Doug Whittle, both of whom Dr. Brauch credits with playing major roles in the effort to find new channels of funding for the Seminary and to reopen old ones. Along with his development team, Dr. Brauch spread the word about the Seminary's mission in the 1990s and, whenever possible, mended fences that had been broken in the near or distant past. The results of their efforts included dramatic increases in annual financial support for the Seminary.

Connections with the Seminary's "glory years" were established through tributes to three of its most beloved and influential professors. Highly esteemed contemporary church historian Martin Marty inaugurated the Robert G. Torbet Lectures in 1991. Unfortunately, Dr. Torbet was unable to attend due to illness. However, Cubby Rutenber was present in the spring of 1992 for the first lecture in his honor, delivered by world-renowned theologian Jürgen Moltmann. Finally, the late Dr. Carl Morgan was memorialized in 1994 through the establishment of the Carl Morgan Visiting Professorship of Biblical Studies.

PROGRAM EXPANSION

As prescribed by its strategic plan, the Seminary launched its Master of Arts in Theological Studies program in 1991. Today it is called the Master of Theological Studies (M.T.S.), and students may choose a concentration in Biblical Studies, Contemporary Theology, Christian Faith and Public Policy, Christian Heritage, Christian Mission, or Christian Counseling.

In 1991, the Seminary also launched a creative program designed to bring quality theological education to the state of West Virginia, where over 10 percent of American Baptists reside. West Virginia native and Board member Robert Matherly, a 1961 graduate of the Seminary, played a key role in organizing the program. President Brauch taught the first class, "Introduction to the

New Testament," attended by forty people. The first seven graduates of the West Virginia program received their degrees in 1999.

A Henry Luce Foundation grant of $260,000 contributed to the launching of the Seminary's second Doctor of Ministry program in 1995. In recognition of contemporary church realities, the Doctor of Ministry in the Renewal of the Church for Mission includes a concentration in urban and minority ministry. The first class of eleven graduated in 1998.

The expansion of programs at the Seminary has contributed to several record enrollments throughout the decade of the 1990s, including the largest entering class in the Seminary's history in 1999 (not counting the first year,

TOP:
DOUG WHITTLE RETURNED TO HIS ALMA MATER IN 1990 AS DIRECTOR OF ALUMNI/AE AND CHURCH RELATIONS, AND HE HELPED RESTORE IT TO FINANCIAL HEALTH.

BOTTOM:
CUBBY RUTENBER (FAR RIGHT) WAS ON HAND IN 1992 FOR THE INAUGURATION OF A LECTURESHIP IN HIS HONOR. HE IS SHOWN HERE WITH PRESIDENT MANFRED BRAUCH, JÜRGEN MOLTMANN, AND CUBBY'S WIFE, DURON.

when all applicants were admitted). Much of this credit belongs to Admissions Director Steve Hutchison. No one through the Seminary's seventy-five years has logged more telephone hours on behalf of the Seminary. In part because of the thirteen years he served as a pastor prior to coming to the Seminary, he brings a pastor's heart to his work, something greatly valued by the many he has recruited through the years. The Admission Office's Exploring Christian Ministries Conference, held annually in March, has resulted in many students enrolling at the Seminary, even though its main purpose is to help women and men interpret God's call on their lives.

BUMPS IN THE ROAD

Despite the Seminary's remarkable progress during the Brauch years, the road was not always smooth. Without doubt, the low point of Dr. Brauch's presidency came in 1995 with the financial collapse of the Foundation for New Era Philanthropy. The Seminary was among the hundreds of educational, church, parachurch, and humanitarian organizations that had been drawn into a relationship with the Foundation, which, as it turned out, was operating based on fraud.

In the expectation of matching funds from anonymous donors who did not exist, the Seminary had $1 million invested with the Foundation at the time of its collapse. As a result, Dr. Brauch and his leadership team had to take the painful step of cutting salaries of Seminary employees across the board. Among the other results were delays in faculty and staff additions, as well as deferred building maintenance and capital improvements.

Fortunately, because of a wise and capable bankruptcy judge and the willingness of the affected organizations to cooperate in a spirit of Christian unity instead of turning to litigation, much of the money—nearly $900,000 in the case of the Seminary—was recovered.

President Brauch also had to deal with controversy over the 1996 release of a Seminary "Policy on Human Sexuality and Moral Conduct." In part because of the potential implications for academic freedom, some members of the faculty opposed the move. However, the president, with the support of the Board of

TOP:
ADMISSIONS DIRECTOR STEVE HUTCHISON (RIGHT), SHOWN HERE IN THE EARLY 1990S WITH POPULAR NEWSPAPER COLUMNIST AND EASTERN SEMINARY STUDENT CHUCK STONE, ENABLED THE SEMINARY TO ACHIEVE STRONG ENROLLMENTS THROUGHOUT THE DECADE.

BOTTOM:
THE SEMINARY TAKES PRIDE IN ITS ETHNIC DIVERSITY, AS ILLUSTRATED BY THIS 1992 PHOTO TAKEN FOR USE IN AN ADVERTISEMENT. PICTURED ARE ROB MARTIN, CHARLES WEST, FELICIA KUMAR (FROM INDIA), GAIL BAIRD, AND DANIEL PASCOE (FROM MEXICO).

IN PLANNING FOR THE FORWARD IN FAITHFULNESS CAPITAL CAMPAIGN, DOUG WHITTLE CAME UP WITH THE IDEA OF MAKING THE SEMINARY CHAPEL A MORE MULTIPURPOSE FACILITY. THUS, THE 45-YEAR-OLD PEWS WERE DONATED TO A LOCAL CHURCH AND REPLACED WITH COMFORTABLE AND MOVABLE CHAIRS. JERRY MILLEVOI

Directors, felt it was necessary to make a statement because of the increased visibility that issues related to sexuality had achieved in the church at large and particularly within the denomination. Among the stated goals of the policy was "to bear witness to a clear alternative to the confusion and brokenness regarding sexuality and sexual behavior in our time."

The Seminary's policy "affirms an ethic in which sexual union is intended for the covenant of marriage between a man and a woman." It continues, "Scripture is clear in its teaching that heterosexual marriage is the created, normative form of human sexual fulfillment, and that a life of disciplined abstinence is normative outside such a relationship."

In the weeks after the policy was published in the Seminary newsletter *inMinistry*, the president received over one hundred letters, the majority (about 90 percent) of which were strongly supportive.

PRESIDENT BRAUCH, STUDENT MODERATOR RESIDENT JOAN HOPPE-SPINK, AND LONGTIME PROFESSOR GLENN KOCH CUT THE CAKE AT THE 1996 LAUNCHING OF THE FORWARD IN FAITHFULNESS CAPITAL CAMPAIGN. JERRY MILLEVOI

FORWARD IN FAITHFULNESS

Before stepping down from the presidency, Dr. Brauch would oversee the launching and near-completion of a $6.3 million capital campaign. Advancement Vice-president R. Scott Rodin served as campaign director. The campaign's success, which Dr. Brauch credits largely to Dr. Rodin's energetic leadership, would result not only in the significant modernization of the Seminary campus, but also in the fiscal stability the institution had long been seeking.

THIS IS HOW
THE LECTURE HALL IN THE BASE-
MENT OF THE CHAPEL BUILDING LOOKED
BEFORE, DURING, AND AFTER THE CAPITAL
CAMPAIGN, DURING WHICH IT WAS NAMED
THE DANIEL R. WOODRUFF LEARNING
CENTER. PROFESSOR IAN SCOTT MAKES
USE OF THE CENTER'S NEW EQUIPMENT.
PAUL EMMA

THE WOODRUFF FAMILY WAS PRESENT FOR
THE DEDICATION IN DECEMBER OF 1997.
KATHY FURLONG

Tony Campolo, one of the Seminary's most widely known and most prolific alumni, was the keynote speaker at the Forward in Faithfulness kickoff dinner in September of 1996. In the spring and early summer of 1999, the Seminary community celebrated the success of the campaign, as signified by $6.57 million in contributions and commitments

from 1,736 sources. Among the gifts was a $600,000 challenge grant from the Kresge Foundation, which put campaign giving over the top.

Among the major improvements to the Seminary was the complete transformation of the lecture hall in Doane Hall into a comfortable lecture hall, fully equipped with the latest in modern technology. Major funding for this project came from Marcia ('84) and Paul Woodruff, who wanted to honor a son who died at age sixteen. The Daniel R. Woodruff Learning Center was dedicated in December of 1997.

Among the other capital renovations was the creation of the Koinonia Center in the veranda of Palmer Hall. The Koinonia Center will for many years serve as a comfortable and attractive gathering place for community-wide fellowship. Additional capital improvements included the building of Founders Bookstore, complete rebuilding and modernization of resident student kitchens and dining rooms, renovation of the Gordon Baker Dining Room, and the equipping of the Guffin Lecture Hall with technology similar to what had been installed in the Woodruff Learning Center.

The Forward in Faithfulness campaign also resulted in $800,000 for endowed scholarships. Of this total, over $500,000 was raised to establish twenty-two named scholarships. An additional $200,000 was designated for two special funds: Teaching Excellence and Student Enrichment, both of which will contribute to the Seminary's charter goals of academic excellence.

Though he was president at the launching of the capital campaign, Dr. Brauch would not be at the helm for the celebration of its success. In stating his desire to return to his first love of teaching, the president quoted the prophet Jeremiah: "There is a burning fire shut up in my bones, and I cannot hold it in." Dr. Brauch's resignation took effect as of June 30, 1997.

A PRESBYTERIAN PRESIDENT

Though he didn't know it in 1993, President Brauch was the one responsible for bringing his successor to Eastern Seminary. Dr. R. Scott Rodin was named acting president in 1997, and at first declined to be a candidate for the permanent position largely because of his denominational affiliation with the Presbyterian Church. But during his year as acting president, he became convinced that it was possible for a non-Baptist to faithfully represent a Baptist seminary within its denominational family and to the larger church and academic community. Encouraged by many within the Seminary community, he allowed his name to be considered. On May 2, 1999, Dr. Rodin was appointed by a unanimous vote of the Board as Eastern Seminary's eleventh president.

Among his priorities early in his tenure has been building relationships between and among Baptists. According to longtime New Testament professor Glenn Koch, "Scott has been able to bring Baptist groups together in a way that many Baptist presidents before him were not." This was exemplified by the 1999 conference "Baptists Together," co-sponsored by the Seminary.

Professor Tom McDaniel believes that Dr. Rodin's Presbyterianism may be working to his advantage: "With a Baptist, people may take some

EASTERN SEMINARY'S TENTH AND ELEVENTH PRESIDENTS, MANFRED BRAUCH AND SCOTT RODIN, TEAMED UP TO TAKE THE SEMINARY TO NEW HEIGHTS AT THE CLOSE OF THE SECOND MILLENNIUM.
JERRY MILLEVOI

IN 1998, THE SEMINARY'S FACULTY ENJOYED
A COMMUNITY-BUILDING EXPERIENCE IN PERU,
THE NATIVE LAND OF PROFESSOR ESCOBAR.

things for granted. But a non-Baptist is more likely to work at building relationships."

Dr. Rodin's idea for a faculty "cross-cultural immersion" experience in Peru illustrated not only his commitment to the understanding of urban and cross-cultural ministry realities, but also his desire for faculty to have fellowship together and to develop a common sense of mission. The 1999 appointments of three African American persons to the Board of Directors—Delores Brisbon, Albert G. Davis, and Violet L. Fisher—demonstrated his commitment to minority representation at the highest levels of Seminary leadership.

The excitement with which President Rodin describes his hopes and plans for Eastern Seminary is not unlike the sense of optimism that characterized the Seminary in its earliest days. At the dawn of the third millennium, the Seminary is in the midst of a major, institution-wide reorganization process that has the potential to redefine seminary education and its delivery for the next generation.

The "organizational chart" at the Seminary will become less hierarchical and more team oriented. President Rodin confidently predicts that the Seminary's revised, interdisciplinary curriculum will be "radically different, unlike any Seminary curriculum we have ever seen."

Institutions typically take such radical steps out of desperation, perhaps the need to attract more students or more funding. But seventy-five years after it was founded, the Seminary is operating out of a position of strength. The catalyst behind the changes is the recognition that the church is losing influence in the society.

The Seminary is not content to rest on its current strength, but desires instead, as it did at its beginning, to be a leader, to forge ahead and break new ground in the process of re-envisioning what it will take in the Third Millennium to share the whole gospel with the whole world through whole persons. Paying tribute to his predecessor, President Rodin acknowledges, "Every thing we are able to do today is a result of the solid foundation we inherited from President Brauch."

Throughout most of the decade of the 1990s, the Seminary was fortunate to have three African American professors as part of its faculty: J. Deotis Roberts, Gerald R. Thomas, and Leah Gaskin Fitchue. Their presence has enabled the Seminary community to strive toward higher levels of sensitivity on issues related to ethnic diversity. Both inside and outside the classroom, they served as role models to all students, but particularly to the Seminary's African American population.

Dr. Roberts, who is among the architects of Black Theology, has moved on to finish his career at Duke University. In 1999, Dr. Fitchue accepted the position of dean with the Interdenominational Theological Center in Atlanta.

UPPER RIGHT:
PROFESSOR J. DEOTIS
ROBERTS. JERRY MILLEVOI

LOWER RIGHT:
PROFESSOR LEAH GASKIN
FITCHUE. PAUL EMMA

LOWER LEFT:
PROFESSOR GERALD R.
THOMAS. JERRY MILLEVOI

POISED FOR THE FUTURE

On its seventy-fifth birthday, Eastern Baptist Theological Seminary appears poised for a future at least as strong and vibrant as its past. Such

W hen Old Testament professor Tom McDaniel retires in the year 2001, it will bring to three the number of "institutions" the Seminary has lost since 1997. Glenn Koch, Tom McDaniel, and Vince deGregoris represent a total of over ninety years of teaching at Eastern Seminary, from which all three graduated.

Including his time at the College, Dr. Koch served the Seminary for forty-two years before his retirement in 1999. He was the protégé of "Mr. Eastern," Dr. Carl Morgan, whom Dr. Koch replaced in 1969 as professor of New Testament Studies and Greek. Like his mentor, Glenn maintained many interests outside the classroom, including birdwatching, archaeology, computers, oil painting, and music. Dr. Koch began leading tours of the Holy Land in 1973. Students' love and respect for their professor was exemplified by the gift of the class of '99: the remodeling and combining of classrooms five and six, which were then named "Koch Hall."

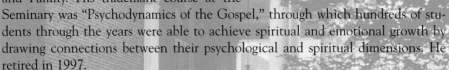

Returning to the Seminary in 1978, Dr. deGregoris helped launch—and for many years directed—the Seminary's Doctor of Ministry program in Ministry to Marriage and Family. His trademark course at the Seminary was "Psychodynamics of the Gospel," through which hundreds of students through the years were able to achieve spiritual and emotional growth by drawing connections between their psychological and spiritual dimensions. He retired in 1997.

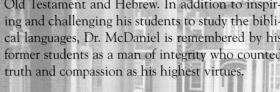

After spending several years on the mission field in Japan, Dr. McDaniel returned to his alma mater in 1969 to succeed W. Everett Griffiths as professor of Old Testament and Hebrew. In addition to inspiring and challenging his students to study the biblical languages, Dr. McDaniel is remembered by his former students as a man of integrity who counted truth and compassion as his highest virtues.

UPPER RIGHT:
PROFESSOR THOMAS F. MCDANIEL. JERRY MILLEVOI

LOWER RIGHT:
PROFESSOR GLENN KOCH. PAUL EMMA

LEFT:
PROFESSOR VINCE DEGREGORIS. PAUL EMMA

confidence begins with the Board of Directors. Many who have been associated with the Seminary for a long time believe that the Board is as strong as it has ever been. Trustees' commitment to the Seminary was demonstrated by their 100 percent participation in the Forward in Faithfulness capital campaign, resulting in nearly $2 million worth of support.

Board Chairman Stanley Nodder, Jr., whose father graduated from the Seminary in 1930, is uniquely qualified for this position, given his experience as a teacher, a pastor, and an investment broker. Most importantly, he is serving his alma mater for the best of all reasons, namely, because he feels he owes Eastern Seminary a debt of gratitude for all it has done for him. A member of the first graduating class of Eastern Baptist College in 1952, Dr. Nodder went on to earn degrees from the Seminary and, based on a Seminary scholarship, from the University of Pennsylvania.

The Seminary has in place an energetic, visionary, and eminently capable president, surrounded by talented people who are in tune with the guiding vision. It was his excitement about the Seminary's future that prompted alumnus Phil Elmore ('85) to return to his alma mater in 1999 as vice president for Advancement. A few years earlier, alumnus Merrit Marsango had done the same thing, returning to the Seminary as director of Seminary Relations and has since become director of Development. Unlike the 1980s, the Seminary is now in the habit of ending each year with a balanced budget.

A faculty that already was top-notch has been strengthened by the recent additions of Dr. Brauch as Maxwell Professor of Biblical Theology and New Testament professor Craig S. Keener, whom predecessor Glenn Koch describes as a "consummate scholar and prolific writer."

And so it was with good reason that Professor McDaniel recently said to group of newly enrolled students: "You are coming to Eastern Seminary at a time when it is at its best."

STANLEY NODDER, JR., WHO FOLLOWED HIS FATHER'S FOOTSTEPS TO EASTERN SEMINARY, CHAIRS WHAT SOME BELIEVE IS THE STRONGEST BOARD OF DIRECTORS IN THE SEMINARY'S HISTORY.
JERRY MILLEVOI.

In addition to raising money for endowed scholarships, the Forward in Faithfulness campaign provided a new bookstore as well as the Koinonia Center to the Seminary community as a comfortable place for fellowship and relaxation. The Gordon Baker Dining Room got a facelift, and the Guffin Lecture Hall was equipped with modern technology, demonstrated here by Professor McDaniel. Paul Emma

1. MOST OF THE SEMINARY'S FEMALE FACULTY CONVERGED FOR THIS PHOTO IN THE EARLY 1990s: MELODY MAZUK, CAROL SCHRECK, LEAH GASKIN FITCHUE, RUTH HENNESSEY, AND ELOUISE RENICH FRASER. JERRY MILLEVOI

2 & 3. TWO OF THE SEMINARY'S MOST RECENT ADDITIONS TO THE BOARD: ALBERT G. DAVIS AND DELORES BRISBON.

4. MEMBERS OF THE SEMINARY STAFF IN THE MID-1990s: SEATED (OR LEANING) IN FRONT: BILL LONG, FELICIA KUMAR, KATHY FURLONG, GAYLE LOVETT, NANCY ADAMS, GISELE CHURN, KATHY WHITTLE, MERRIT MARSANGO, AND RANDY FRAME. STANDING IN BACK: DAVID HERSH, ESTHER GEORGE, SANDI MEYERS, BERYL RUSSELL, JOAN WOOTERS, LORI POTTS, GAIL BAIRD, LORRAINE MATHEWSON, MOSES KUMAR, BARBARA BEAUDRY, RICH WHITE, VILMA STILP, JANICE MARSANGO, AND SHERI MAGNESS. PAUL EMMA

5. REGISTRAR RUTH MCFARLAND'S SERVICE TO THE SEMINARY SPANS OVER THREE DECADES.

IN 1999, A CROSS REPLACED THE WEATHER VANE ATOP THE SEMINARY'S CHAPEL BUILDING. THIS WOULD NOT HAVE HAPPENED IN AN EARLIER ERA, WHEN MOST CONSERVATIVE BAPTISTS FELT THAT A CROSS SYMBOLIZED CATHOLICISM.

KATHY FURLONG

praise & PROMISE

1925-2000

Eastern Baptist Theological Seminary

75

TOP TO BOTTOM:

THE COMMUNITY GATHERED TO DEDICATE THE NEW KOINONIA CENTER. PAUL EMMA

AMONG THE CONTEMPORARY SEMINARY TRADITIONS IS FOR FACULTY TO COOK AND SERVE THE SENIOR DINNER. WORKING HERE—OR AT LEAST PRETENDING TO BE WORKING—ARE ERIC OHLMANN, STEVE HUTCHISON, AND MELODY MAZUK.

GRADUATES OF THE FIRST DOCTOR OF MINISTRY RENEWAL CLASS AT THE 1998 COMMENCEMENT. LEFT TO RIGHT ARE MARK MCCLEARY, SILAS M. TOWNSEND, RODNEY ELLIS KING, AND RICHARD A. DENT. JERRY MILLEVOI

THE GRADUATING CLASS OF 1997. JERRY MILLEVOI

Conclusion: Timeless Values

F or many years after it was founded in 1925, Eastern Seminary was widely referred to as the "Miracle of Faith." The story of its origins and of its fast growth into prominence is indeed a remarkable one.

So much has changed since those early days. As we have seen, in that whirlwind first year, all applicants were admitted. Tuition was free, room and board came to $6 a week, and full-time professors were paid a whopping $3,600 in annual salary. In the early years, students wore suits or nice dresses to class, ate their meals together, and sang after dinner as they washed the dishes. When the school opened its doors, the library had all of two volumes. Today, it has over 130,000. Times have changed indeed.

Perhaps more remarkable than the extent to which times have changed, however, is the extent to which they have remained the same. The professors have changed, as have the programs and the names of the degrees. The theological issues debated between so-called conservatives and progressives have changed as well. Yet the Seminary's original doctrinal basis, only slightly amended, remains intact as a firm foun-

eleven

CHARLES T. BALL, THE FIRST PRESIDENT.

R. SCOTT RODIN, THE ELEVENTH PRESIDENT.

dation and a guiding light. And virtually every value and ideal, every instinct, dream and goal that the Seminary holds dear in the year 2000 can be traced to the seeds planted by its founders in 1925.

DOORS OPEN TO ALL

Far from being an elitist institution, the Seminary in the beginning opened its doors to all who wanted to learn and who had a heart to serve Christ. Thus, throughout its history, even those who lacked academic credentials had access to high-quality biblical and theological knowledge, as well as to practical ministry training, through such avenues as evening school or correspondence courses.

Eastern College exists today because the Seminary in the beginning welcomed everyone. In 1926, tutors were hired to address students' educational deficiencies. This turned into the Sub-Junior Department,

which in 1932 became the Collegiate Division, which in 1952 became Eastern Baptist College.

This same urging dominated the Seminary's Evening School for Laymen in the 1970s, a precursor to the Eastern School of Christian Ministry (ESCM), a certificate program begun in 1983. As the new century begins, over 250 students are enrolled in ESCM at five Greater Philadelphia locations.

A COMMITMENT TO SCHOLARSHIP

From its beginning, the Seminary was committed to high standards of biblical and theological scholarship. President de Blois's efforts to achieve and maintain those standards have been well-documented. In a time when foundational affirmations of Christian faith were being challenged or denied, the Seminary's founders wisely recognized that running away from the issues was not the answer. Instead, they aspired to attract people of faith who had both the ability and the commitment to engage their theological opponents in the debates of the day.

In the 1960s, a survey of 1,500 Eastern Seminary alums conducted by Dean Walter Bruce Davis revealed that 410 had gone on for further study, and of these, 102 had earned doctoral degrees. Carl Morgan, Cubby Rutenber, William Powers, Arthur Crabtree, and in more modern

times Glenn Koch, Tom McDaniel, Manfred Brauch, Elouise Renich Fraser, and J. Deotis Roberts are among the many who through the years have integrated ardent faith and expert scholarship. Now, as then, the leadership of Eastern Seminary recognizes the high importance of Bible and theological knowledge.

MINISTRY IN ACTION

Yet from the beginning, the education students received at Eastern Seminary was never intended to remain confined to the proverbial "ivory tower." Unlike other seminaries at the time, Eastern emphasized a study of the English Bible out of a commitment to make the gospel relevant to local congregations. Thus it is fitting that the James A. Maxwell Chair of English Bible was the first professorial chair to be endowed.

The Seminary began out of a concern for upholding the foundations of the Christian faith, but the activities of the early years collectively proclaimed that the Seminary's mission went far beyond merely a religion of right words or proper doctrine. William W. Adams, who chaired the original curriculum, was well known for his emphasis on the social implications of the gospel. Under Professor Livingston, who in 1930 became director of Evangelism, students were required to turn in monthly reports detailing their

endeavors in practical fields of service. Often students went straight from class to the streets of Philadelphia to preach the gospel. They played basketball with young people and then witnessed to them. They visited hospitals, comforted the sick, and provided practical aid to those in need.

The Seminary's emphasis on field work constituted a new mold in the delivery of theological education. Carl Morgan, "Mr. Eastern," was a Rhodes scholar, but scholarship meant nothing to him unless it had relevance for serving the church. Dr. Morgan literally wrote the book on field work: *The Status of Field Work in the Theological Seminaries of the United States*. This book, published in 1942, helped put the Seminary on the map as an innovative institution. Over twenty theological seminaries came to the Seminary for landmark conferences on field work in 1946 and again in 1947.

Now, as then, Eastern Seminary students are immersed in the "whole gospel." They understand that the message of Jesus' saving love cannot be separated from a commitment to serve, from a hand stretched out to those in need or from taking a stand for justice. It is no accident that the offices of Evangelicals for Social Action have for many years been located at the Seminary.

The Seminary's location, while technically in the suburbs, is not nearly so suburban as it was when the school moved here in 1940. This proximity to an urban center, along with the commitment to urban ministry, is a source of attraction to many students today.

THEOLOGICAL BALANCE

The Seminary's founders staunchly believed that the quest to be both conservative and progressive was the right path to take, even though it was not always an easy path. It would have been far easier, including for purposes of raising funds, to set forth a clear, detailed, immutable system of beliefs and acceptable practices. The founders recognized, however, the ease with which debatable secondary doctrinal beliefs could be

JOHN B. CHAMPION, PROFESSOR OF CHRISTIAN DOCTRINE.

ELOUISE RENICH FRASER, PROFESSOR OF SYSTEMATIC THEOLOGY/ASSOCIATE DEAN.
JERRY MILLEVOI

RONALD J. SIDER, PROFESSOR OF THEOLOGY AND CULTURE.
JERRY MILLEVOI

wrongly confused with the foundations of the gospel. They took into account the fact that intelligent Christians whose faith could not be questioned disagreed on some issues.

And so they ventured down a different path, one that would be solidly grounded in a conservative doctrinal basis but that allowed for the possibility of new directions, of change, progress, and growth. As the 1959–60 catalog put it, the Seminary maintained "that although truth is fixed and eternal, man's apprehension of it is finite and hence subject to continual improvement. That truth may be better apprehended is the reason for encouraging all types of research."

The commitment to be both conservative and progressive led to tensions from the very beginning. Board members, as well as faculty, did not always see eye-to-eye on which ideas or textbooks remained within the boundaries of acceptable theology. This theme recurs at points throughout the Seminary's history, and it does so because the Seminary early on made the commitment to entertain new thoughts and ideas, and through the years it has accepted the painstaking responsibility that comes with it, namely that of separating the "wheat" from the "chaff."

For its refusal, historically, to become captive to the ideologies of Left or Right, Eastern Seminary has been willing to pay a price. From the beginning and through the years it has been deemed—simultaneously— "too liberal" or "too conservative," depending of course on from whence the charge is hurled. This continues to be true today.

The negative fallout from such an approach is not limited to a hampering of public relations success or of the ability to raise money. At times through the years, careers have been threatened and feelings have been hurt. Yet there have been no all-out "witch hunts," or at least, as far as can be determined, no one ended up getting burned at the stake. Love, truth, and progress have found a way to co-exist, each having found a voice in the Seminary's expression of its corporate faith.

Now, as then, the Seminary quite consciously embraces a centrist approach, grounded solidly in the very heart of its dearest values and most treasured traditions. In the Summer 1999 issue of *inMinistry*, President Rodin writes, "If we are to be labeled, Eastern Seminary is a centrist evangelical institution. The challenge for an institution like us is delivering our message with both clarity and passion. These belong more easily to those on the extremes. Centrists seldom hold protest marches, use vitriolic language, demonize their opponents or draw lines in the sand. We are not fist shakers or rally organizers. We eschew the indoctrination of the right and the relativism of the left."

He goes on to state that the church's history "has witnessed swings right and left," but has "proven itself best when it has found the balance in the middle." In an effort to move the Seminary to a new level, the president is seeking to lead the charge toward a more passionate, unapologetic expression of the institution's centrist position.

A VISIONARY SPIRIT

The Seminary's founders had no awareness of any limitations on what God could accomplish through their plans. Even with no money, no buildings, and no teachers, they proceeded in faith. The Seminary opened its doors offering virtually every degree program anyone could think of: ten to be exact. Contemporary institutional planners would have cringed. In contrast, the 1959–60 catalog listed only three degrees, two in Theology, and one in Christian Education.

Clearly the founders' reach extended their capacity to grasp and hold on. But they were willing to take the risk of reaching high. They were not content with third-rate dreams. And because they reached so high, what they were ultimately able to grab onto was plenty high enough.

Now, as then, a visionary spirit permeates Eastern Seminary and its leadership, as evidenced by the reorganization process in which it is now engaged. Not content with business as usual, the Seminary instead is aspiring to reinvent graduate theological education not just for its own sake, but also as a model for all institutions with similar values and goals.

ECUMENICAL, BUT DISTINCTIVELY BAPTIST

The fact that the founders limited their theological commitments to the essentials of the Christian faith made it virtually inevitable that the Seminary would end up working alongside Christians from other denominations who held the same basic beliefs. Though Baptist students have always comprised the single biggest denominational grouping at the Seminary, the school has never been

LEFT:
DAVID L. JAMISON, PROFESSOR OF PHILOSOPHY OF RELIGION.

RIGHT:
HORACE O. RUSSELL, PROFESSOR OF HISTORICAL THEOLOGY AND DEAN OF CHAPEL.

narrowly Baptist. Early in the Seminary's history, its doors were open to non-Baptist students. In the 1970s, it welcomed non-Baptists to the Board and to the faculty. In 1998, the Seminary officially welcomed a non-Baptist president.

Yet the Seminary's commitment to serve all believers has been balanced by a sense of loyalty to the Baptist denomination to which it is related and by a commitment to uphold distinctively Baptist convictions. Though non-Baptists serve on the Board, bylaws mandate that a majority of trustees be Baptist. Among the commitments made by Dr. Rodin on becoming president was to represent the Seminary in Baptist circles and to promote its Baptist identity. These are commitments that he has taken very seriously.

A PROPHETIC VOICE

The Seminary's commitment to theological moderation has never meant that it advocates moderation when it comes to taking a stand for justice. In twentieth-century America, issues of justice have been defined largely around the nation's unjust treatment of African American people. On this count, it must be acknowledged that the Seminary's past is far from pure.

To be sure, while many Christian educational institutions openly denied admission to black students, such was never the case at Eastern Seminary. Also to its credit, African American guest lecturers for whom the doors of other institutions were closed found open doors at Eastern.

The fact remains, however, that during the first third of the Seminary's history, African American men and women were not permitted to live on campus. According to Dr. Rutenber, that changed under President Guffin, who ironically is the only one of the Seminary's presidents who came from the South.

Nor were black students, or black families from the area, allowed to use the campus swimming pool. Cubby Rutenber may have officially integrated the pool in the 1940s, but because of the prevalent social attitudes at the Seminary and in its surrounding community, the pool was, for all intents and purposes, off limits to black people for many more years.

It can be argued that the Seminary was merely reflecting the larger culture of which it was a part. While that may help provide perspective, it does not excuse attitudes and behaviors that can only be described as racist, with all the negative connotations that accompany that ugly term. No explanation or qualification has ever been compelling enough to relieve the Seminary of the need to repent, seek forgiveness, and pursue healing, all of which it has attempted to do.

And yet even in the midst of the ignorance and prejudice of the past could be heard prophetic voices calling for justice, calling for change. Though these voices were not always heeded, neither were they fully suppressed. Dr. Rutenber was able to challenge entire generations of seminary students to examine their lives, values, and priorities in ways that changed their hearts and minds.

One of the Seminary's founders, Ralph L. Mayberry, through the years stood like a giant against the cultural tides of prejudice and injustice. When Japanese-Americans were being imprisoned during World War II, he fought the FBI, prepared to wear such labels as "subversive" and "un-American."

On one occasion, an FBI officer came to Dr. Mayberry's office to check on the character of a particular Japanese-American. He asked Dr. Mayberry if he'd ever heard the man in question swear his loyalty to the United States. Mayberry responded in anger, "No, I haven't and neither have I heard you." The fact that twenty years after his death Dr. Mayberry's name is still revered by Japanese-Americans on the West Coast is an apt testimony to the values he upheld.

WILBER T. ELMORE, PROFESSOR OF MISSIONARY AND CHRISTIAN HISTORY.

ERIC H. OHLMANN, DEAN AND PROFESSOR OF CHRISTIAN HERITAGE. RON STEWART PHOTOGRAPHY

JAMES A. MAXWELL, FIRST CHAIRMAN OF THE BOARD

MANFRED T. BRAUCH, JAMES A. MAXWELL PROFESSOR OF BIBLICAL THEOLOGY.

LEFT TO RIGHT:
GEORGE W. SWOPE,
PROFESSOR OF EVANGELISM.

THORNLEY B. WOOD
PROFESSOR OF MISSIOLOGY J.
SAMUEL ESCOBAR. JERRY MILLEVOI

LEFT TO RIGHT:
L. SARLE BROWN, DIRECTOR OF
DEPARTMENT OF CHRISTIAN MUSIC.

WILL BARNES, ASSOCIATE
PROFESSOR OF CHRISTIAN
MINISTRIES/DIRECTOR OF MARRIAGE
AND FAMILY DOCTOR OF MINISTRY.
PAUL EMMA

Thankfully, voices of justice eventually won out. There was a time in the Seminary's history when some were embarrassed or ashamed about the presence of African American students. Today, the 30-plus percent of African American students constitutes a source of healthy pride. And the Seminary's leadership is committed to insuring that persons of color are well represented at all levels.

As for its treatment of women, historically the Seminary's past is less tainted, though it still leaves much to be desired. The founders had no qualms about female instructors. A woman was among the Board members during the first year. The first librarian was a woman, and no female student was ever denied entrance to any program of the Seminary because of her gender.

To be sure, women were an "issue" in the early years, as suggested by various documents and records. Reading between the lines of some of this material, however, one could easily conclude that the problem was not so much with women as it was with men who had trouble staying away from the women. (Some things never change.)

In any event, Dr. de Blois reported in the 1930s that "for some time the question of the admission of women students to the regular courses of the Seminary had been agitating the minds of quite a number of officers and friends of the Institution."

The topic was the object of spirited debate at the annual Board meeting in 1931, which led to the formation of a committee to consider it. The result, President de Blois reported, was "that the doors of the Seminary should be open quite as widely and as graciously for the entrance of competent women students as for the entrance of competent male students. This undoubtedly is a broad and sane and thoroughly modern policy. . . . Although there may not be in the near future any large number of young women seeking preparation for the work of the Christian ministry as pastors, there is surely no reason why a theological seminary should not allow equal privileges to women and to men. . . ." Even today, such a statement would be considered radical or liberal in some circles.

Such a commitment notwithstanding, there is ample evidence to suggest that throughout its early history the Seminary did not do enough to push against the restraints imposed by a patriarchal culture. But there were positive seeds sown in the beginning, and over the last two and a half decades the Seminary has sought to stand against the tide of the culture, including some segments of church culture, by affirming and respecting the full and unqualified presence of women in ministry. As dean in the 1980s Dr. Brauch developed a new policy statement affirming the equality of men and women and of their calling into all the ministries of Christ. Inclusive language is required for academic papers. Roughly half of the Seminary's students are women, and the Seminary is committed to making sure these students have the mentors and role models they need to respond faithfully to God's call on their lives.

Mistakes, misunderstandings, and insensitivity sometimes slowed the quest for justice and fairness. But voices of progress, hope, justice and love won out. One such voice was Dr. Mayberry's. In eulogizing Ralph L. Mayberry in 1980, Dr. Jitsuo Morikawa called him "a man of intolerance and impatience who swept through life like a whirlwind." Morikawa added that had Dr. Mayberry's "intolerance been misdirected, he would have ended up an impossible bigot, but transformed by the grace of God his restless impatience became the motivating force of a powerful life that plowed through time like a juggernaut."

According to Morikawa, Ralph Mayberry had "a contemptuous intolerance for cowardice and timidity," a "searing, burning intolerance for injustice, whether against Blacks, or Hispanics or Asians or Caucasians," and "a scorching intolerance for duplicity and dishonesty." The Seminary in the year 2000 aspires to be so intolerant.

• A commitment to serve the church of Jesus Christ and to uphold the essential claims of the gospel.

• A willingness to find a place for all who want to learn and serve, combined with a strong sense of loyalty to Baptist traditions.

• A commitment to quality scholarship that serves as a foundation for sound, vital, proactive ministry, scholarship that is captive not to ideological agendas, but is committed to discovering God's truth.

• A visionary spirit.

• A willingness to take a stand for justice and righteousness on both the personal and social levels.

• In sum, a burning desire to proclaim the whole gospel to the whole world through whole persons.

These are the ideals that have guided the Eastern Baptist Theological Seminary for seventy-five years. And from all indications, they are the same, timeless values that will accompany the Seminary in the years ahead.

TOP:
THE GRADUATING CLASS OF 1928.

BOTTOM:
THE GRADUATING CLASS OF 1998.
JERRY MILLEVOI

Appendices

A SEMINARY TIMELINE

March 19, 1925—Six ministers meet at the Philadelphia headquarters of the American Baptist Publication Society for the official founding of the Eastern Baptist Theological Seminary. Charles T. Ball is selected as president.

May 1925—A gift of stock holdings worth $500,000 enables the Seminary to purchase buildings on Philadelphia's Rittenhouse Square and to hire faculty.

September 22, 1925—Eastern Seminary opens its doors to students. Before the year ends, over one hundred will enroll.

May 1926—The Seminary graduates its first class of eleven members. The Board elects Austen K. de Blois as the Seminary's second president.

1931—The Board votes to allow non-Baptist students to enter the Seminary.

1932—The Collegiate Division is officially established.

1936—Gordon Palmer becomes the Seminary's third president.

1939—The Seminary purchases the Green Hill Farms Hotel in Overbrook, on the edge of the city.

1940—In February, the Seminary moves to its new Overbrook campus, where it would remain for the remainder of the millennium.

1945—The twentieth anniversary capital campaign raises $500,000.

1950—Gilbert Guffin begins duties as the Seminary's fourth president.

1951—The Curtis Lee Laws Memorial Chapel/William Howard Doane Hall are built and dedicated thanks to the generosity of Marguerite Treat Doane.

1952—Eastern Baptist College is founded as a separate institution and is located at the former Walton estate *Walmarthon* in St. Davids, eight miles west of the Seminary campus. The Women's Auxiliary organization is begun.

1954—Both the Seminary and the College are granted much sought-after accreditation from the American Association of Theological Schools and the Middle States Association.

1956—The Swartley Lectureship series is inaugurated at the Seminary.

1957—The Seminary gets a new building addition to serve as its library, thanks to money raised by the thirtieth anniversary capital campaign. The building is dedicated in 1958.

1961—Thomas McDormand becomes the fifth president of Eastern Seminary.

1962—The Program for Progress capital campaign is launched with a goal of raising $1.1 million.

1967—The Master of Divinity (M.Div.) replaces the Bachelor of Divinity (B.D.) as the primary degree for ministry preparation.

1968—J. Lester Harnish becomes the sixth president of Eastern Seminary.

1969—The Board of Directors is reorganized to allow for as many as nine non-Baptists out of a total of thirty-six Board members.

1971—Eastern Baptist College is renamed Eastern College. About a decade before beginning his tenure as U.S. Surgeon General, C. Everett Koop becomes the first non-Baptist Board member in the Seminary's history.

1973—Daniel E. Weiss becomes the Seminary's seventh president; the Seminary launches its first Doctor of Ministry program. The Ralph L. Mayberry Chair of Evangelism and Pastoral Ministry is inaugurated.

1978—Ron Sider becomes the first non-Baptist full-time faculty member.

1980—Ralph Mayberry, the last surviving member of the group of six who founded Eastern Seminary, dies at the age of ninety-two. The Seminary launches a Doctor of Ministry program in Ministry to Marriage and Family.

1981—The Frank B. Mitchell Lectureship is begun as a yearly celebration of Black History.

1983—Robert Seiple becomes the eighth president of Eastern Seminary.

1985—The Seminary's original Doctor of Ministry program is discontinued.

1985—For the first time in its history, part-time students at the Seminary outnumber full-time students.

1987—The process of dividing the Seminary and College into two, administratively distinct schools begins. Robert Campbell becomes the ninth president in the Seminary's history, and Roberta Hestenes becomes the first president to serve only Eastern College.

1990—After serving for a year as acting president, Manfred T. Brauch is chosen in March to serve as the Seminary's tenth president. Four months later, an original Mozart is among a handful of long-forgotten classical music manuscripts discovered in a Seminary safe. They were auctioned off for about $1.5 million.

1991—The Robert G. Torbet Lectureship in Church History is inaugurated. The Seminary launches an extension program in the state of West Virginia.

1992—The Culbert G. Rutenber Lectureship is inaugurated in honor of one of the Seminary's most celebrated professors.

1993—The governing Boards of Eastern College and Eastern Seminary are separated; Stanley Nodder, Jr., becomes chairman of the Seminary's Board.

1994—The Seminary honors "Mr. Eastern," Carl Morgan, though the establishment of the Carl Morgan Visiting Professorship of Biblical Studies.

1995—The Seminary launches its Doctor of Ministry (D. Min.) program in the Renewal of the Church for Mission.

1996—The Seminary kicks off its three-year, $6.3 million Forward in Faithfulness capital campaign. Its success results in major capital improvements to the Seminary campus and the establishing of twenty-two endowed scholarships.

1997—President Brauch steps down in order to return to his first love of teaching. R. Scott Rodin is named acting president.

1998—R. Scott Rodin becomes Eastern Seminary's eleventh president and its first non-Baptist leader. He initiates a reorganization process whose goal is to revolutionize the delivery of graduate level theological education.

1999—On June 30, the Forward in Faithfulness campaign officially concludes, having surpassed the $6.3 million goal.

2000—In March, Eastern Baptist Theological Seminary celebrates seventy-five years of faithfulness to the mission of preparing women and men to take the whole gospel to the whole world through whole persons.

PRESIDENTS OF EASTERN BAPTIST THEOLOGICAL SEMINARY

Charles T. Ball—1925–1926
Austen Kennedy de Blois—1926–1936
Gordon Palmer—1936–1948
Gilbert Lee Guffin—1950–1961
Thomas Bruce McDormand—1961–1967
J. Lester Harnish—1968–1972
Henry R. Osgood (Acting)—1972–1973
Daniel E. Weiss—1973–1981
Robert A. Seiple—1983–1987
Robert C. Campbell—1987–1989
Manfred Theophil Brauch—1981–1983 (Acting), 1989 (Acting), 1990–1997
R. Scott Rodin—1997 (Acting), 1998–

Note: In the interim period between Presidents Palmer and Guffin (1948–1950), the Seminary was led by a committee co-chaired by Dean Carl Morgan and Treasurer Harvey Bartle.

SOME PRESIDENTIAL FACTS

• Three of the Seminary's eleven presidents are alumni: Guffin ('35, '38, '41), Harnish ('38, '45), and Campbell ('47, '49, '51, '74).
• The youngest president to take office was Daniel Weiss at the age of thirty-five. The oldest was Robert Campbell at age sixty-three.
• Three presidents were born in other countries: Austen Kennedy de Blois and Thomas Bruce McDormand in Canada and Manfred Theophil Brauch in Germany. (Only vun of zees three, however, hed eh zstrong eggsent.)
• Six of the Seminary's ten former presidents—de Blois, Palmer, Guffin, Harnish, Seiple, and Brauch—continued to serve the Seminary in some official capacity after stepping down. Of these, Presidents Palmer, Guffin, Harnish, and Seiple served for at least a short time on the Seminary's Governing Board. Gilbert Guffin served a total of thirty-nine years on the Board, nine of those years before becoming president. Gordon Palmer served for twenty-eight years on the Board, and Robert Seiple for two. Lester Harnish has served on the Board for fourteen years and is still an emeritus member.
• The last two Seminary presidents—Manfred Theophil Brauch and R. Scott Rodin—are the only presidents to have been chosen from within the ranks of those employed by the Seminary.
• Each of the Seminary's first seven presidents had pastoral experience. Each of its last four presidents have not.

CHAIRMEN OF THE SEMINARY BOARD

Frank M. Goodchild	1925 (March to November)
James A. Maxwell	1925–1939
Charles S. Walton, Jr.	1939–1960
Paul E. Almquist	1960–1970
Frank F. Middleswart	1970–1984
Maurice Workman	1984–1989
Ardell Thomas	1989–1993
Stanley Nodder, Jr.	1993–

THE BOARD OF TRUSTEES

CHARTER MEMBERS

Gordon H. Baker	David Lee Jamison
Charles T. Ball	Curtis Lee Laws
Harry Watson Barras	James A. Maxwell
John E. Briggs (emeritus)	Ralph L. Mayberry
E. B. Dwyer	Frank Earle Parham
Frank M. Goodchild	P. Vanis Slawter
John A. Hainer	Thornley B. Wood

THE BOARD IN THE YEAR 2000

Ronald K. Adams	Thomas J. Ritter
Louise Williams Bishop	R. Scott Rodin (Seminary president)
Delores F. Brisbon	Gus Roman
R. Dandridge Collins	Richard Rusbuldt
Rick Conrad	Earl G. Russell, Sr.
Albert G. Davis, Jr.	William B. Scatchard, Jr.
James M. Dunn	Richard E. Shearer
William T. Dunn	Roberta M. Sherwin
William J. Feeney	Wallace Charles Smith
Violet L. Fisher	Edward Sparkman
John D. Jordan	Cora Sparrowk
Robert E. Matherly	John Todd Stewart
David C. Montgomery	John A. Sundquist
Stanley Nodder, Jr. (chair)	F. Ardell Thomas
Janis Plostnieks	Marcia J. Woodruff
Dorothy Porter	J. Eugene Wright

DIRECTORS EMERITI

Paul E. Almquist	J. Lester Harnish
Abram S. Clemens	Samuel T. Hudson
Conrad J. Fowler	Chester J. Jump, Jr.
Wesley I Evans	Maurice C. Workman

SEMINARY FACULTY ROSTER

Following is a list of those who have taught at Eastern Seminary as full-time faculty or regular instructors. Except for charter professors George Swope and Charles Ball, the list is limited to those who served for at least three years. Lecturers are not included, although if someone served as a faculty member or regular instructor, their years of service as a lecturer are included.

Several of those listed below served in a variety of positions during their time at the Seminary. Only the primary area or areas of specialty are noted. Because Seminary catalogues are among the sources for the information below, the actual dates of service may differ slightly from what is listed.

NAME	YEARS OF SERVICE	AREA OF SPECIALTY
Adams, William W.	1925–1946	New Testament
Anderson, Helen D.	1944–1948	Dean of Women (College Div.)/Christian Education
Ball, Charles T.	1925–1926	Practical Theology
Baker, Nelson B	1951–1971	English Bible
Bakke, Raymond J.	1994–	Urban Mission
Barnes, Will	1995–	Christian Ministries
Barras, Harry Watson	1925–1936	Homiletics
Bartle, Harvey, Jr.	1937–1973	Psychiatry/Psychology
Bender, Thorwald W.	1959–1973	Theology
Bowman, Joseph R.	1936–1969	Music
Brackney, William H.	1986–1989	Dean/Church History
Brauch, Manfred Theophil	1978–	Dean/New Testament
Brown, L. Sarle	1925–1952	Music
Campbell, Robert C.	1987–1989	Biblical Studies
Carson, Josephine B.	1936–1968	Librarian
Champion, John Benjamin	1925–1941	Christian Doctrine
Chartier, Janet	1974–1987	Christian Education
Chartier, Myron R.	1974–1987	Ministry/Director of Doctoral Program
Cooley, Paul B.	1944–1946	English
Costas, Orlando E.	1979–1984	Missiology
Crabtree, Arthur Bamford	1957–1963	Theology
Dalglish, Edward R.	1952–1966	Old Testament/Hebrew
Davis, Walter Bruce	1954–1978	Dean/Missions
de Blois, Austen Kennedy	1926–1945	Practical Theology
deGregoris, Vincent	1978–1997	Pastoral Psychology
Demarest, Charles N.	1925–1930	Music
Elmore, Maud Johnson	1925–1941	Missions
Elmore, Wilber T.	1925–1935	Missions/Church History

Englerth, Gilbert R.	1967–1980	Librarian
Escobar, Juan Samuel	1985–	Missiology
Fitchue, Leah Gaskin	1992–1999	Urban Ministry
Fraser, Elouise Renich	1983–	Theology
Gabelman, Gustave A.	1960–1978	Field Education
Gutierrez, Angel Luis	1987–1989	Pastoral Ministry
Gorham, Donald R.	1930–1942	Christian Education
Griffiths, W. Everett	1930–1952, 1966–1969	Old Testament
Grigolia, Alexander	1946–1967	Anthropology
Gross, Nancy Lammers	1991–	Homiletics
Guffin, Gilbert Lee	1950–1961	Pastoral Theology
Hand, William John	1943–1977	Librarian/Pastoral Counseling
Harnish, J. Lester	1968–1972	Preaching
Harris, Arthur Emerson	1925–1950	Psychology/Bible
Heaton, Ada Beth	1950–1959	Christian Education
Heaton, C. Adrian	1947–1959	Christian Education
Hennessey, Ruth Wegner	1988–1996	Field Education
Henry, Carl F. H.	1969–1973	Theology
Herman, William John	1937–1941	Hebrew
Hester, James D.	1937–1940	Speech
Hutchison, Stephen	1984–	Director of Admissions
Jackson, Herbert Cross	1951–1954	Missions
Jamison, David Lee	1925–1941	Philosophy of Religion
Jones, Irene Ann	1934–1942	Dean of Women/ English
Keener, Craig S.	1999–	New Testament
Koch, Glenn Alan	1961–1999	New Testament/Greek
Leypoldt, Martha	1966–1973	Christian Education
Livingston, Benjamin T.	1930–1941	Evangelism
Mapson, Jesse Wendell	1992–1996	Director of ESCM
Maring, Norman	1948–1978	Dean/Church History
Massee, Jasper C.	1938–1941	Homiletics
Matthews, Harry Alexander	1937–1941	Music
Maxwell, James A.	1926–1948	English Bible
Mazuk, Melody	1992–	Library Director
McDaniel, Thomas Francis	1969–	Old Testament/Hebrew
McDormand, Thomas Bruce	1961–1967	Pastoral Theology
McEllhenney, John G.	1999–	Methodist Studies
McFarland, Ruth	1972–	Registrar
Miller, Douglas James	1970–1990	Christian Social Ethics
Mueller, William Arthur	1936–1945	Church History
Morgan, Carl Hamilton	1929–1969	Dean/New Testament
Ohlmann, Eric Henry	1990–	Dean/Christian Heritage
Ortegon, Samuel M.	1946–1952	Spanish/Sociology
Palmer, Gordon	1936–1948	Pastoral Theology/Homiletics
Parker, Kenneth Russell	1983–1989	Christian Ministry
Paullin, Norman W.	1952–1968	Homiletics
Phelps, Marion Stein	1937–1941	Music
Powers, William Emmett	1941–1969	Theology
Price, Eleanor Brech	1928–1939	Librarian
Ramm, Bernard L.	1974–1978	Theology
Reiff, Evan A.	1946–1950	English
Roberts, James Deotis	1984–1998	Philosophical Theology
Roddy, Clarence S.	1944–1951	English Bible
Rodin, R. Scott	1994–	Theology
Russell, Horace Orlando	1990–	Church History/Dean of Chapel
Rutenber, Culbert G.	1939–1958, 1973–1979	Philosophy of Religion/Ethics
Sahlin, Clarence J.	1962–1966	Christian Education
Schreck, Carol Y.	1980–	Counseling
Schreck, Guenther Peter	1980–	Pastoral Care/Counseling
Scott, Ian J.	1997–	New Testament/Director of ESCM
Shane, Mae Deal	1937–1942	Christian Education
Sider, Ronald James	1978–	Theology
Smith, Wallace Charles	1979–1986	Pastoral Theology
Snyder, Virginia A.	1929–1936	Music (piano)
Stephenson, Esther Todd	1942–1946	Voice
Stilwell, Herbert F.	1926–1930	Evangelism
Sturgis, Russell	1937–1941	Science
Sully, Eva Folsom	1942–1946	Piano
Swope, George W.	1925–1926	Evangelism
Taylor, Barnard Cook	1925–1937	Old Testament
Taylor, Irene Card	1928–1933	Music
Telford, James Haxton	1944–1950	Missions
Thomas, Gerald Lamont	1992–	Preaching
Thompson, William D.	1962–1986	Preaching
Torbet, Robert George	1934–1951	Church History
Trulear, Harold Dean	1987–1990	Church and Society/Black Church Studies
Vanderlip, D. George	1971–1982	English Bible
Veninga, Frank	1970–1978	Executive Vice-President
Ward, Margaret Sherwood	1937–1941	Christian Education
Watson, Deborah E.	1999–	Greek
Williams, Albert G.	1942–1969	Homiletics
Woodard, Marsha Brown	1999–	Christian Ministry
Wool, Peter C.	1999–	Christian Ministry
Wortley, George F.	1926–1930	Religious Education

| Wright, J. Eugene, Jr. | 1973–1982 | Evangelism/Pastoral Ministry |
| Wrighton, William Hazar | 1941–1944 | Homiletics/English Bible |

HONORARY DEGREES AWARDED BY THE SEMINARY

NAME	YEAR	DEGREE
John A. Hainer	1932	D.D.
Benjamin Thomson Livingston	1935	D.D.
Ralph L. Mayberry	1940	D.D.
Albert Hayes Stanton	1940	D.D.
Raymond B. Buker	1943	D.D.
Irene A. Jones	1943	M.R.E.
Virginia Snyder	1945	B.S.M.
William Walter Adams	1946	D.D.
Benjamin P. Browne	1947	D.D.
Archibald T. O. Marks	1948	D.D.
Hubert A. Davidson	1949	D.D.
F. Townley Lord	1951	D.D.
Glenn H. Asquith	1952	D.D.
Oscar Rodriquez	1952	D.D.
John Murray Armstrong	1953	D.D.
Richard Eugene Shearer	1953	D.D.
Frank K. Brasington	1954	D.D.
Winfield Edson	1954	D.D.
Alger W. Geary	1954	D.D.
Elmer Newcomb Bentley	1955	D.D.
Gordon Herman Schroeder	1955	D.D.
Alton Groff Snyder	1955	D.D.
Ronald Kinley Adams	1956	D.D.
Oliver Wallingford Hurst	1956	D.D.
Charles Sumner Lee	1956	D.D.
Eugene Albert Nida	1956	D.D.
Theodore E. Bubeck	1957	D.D.
G. Wesley Huber	1957	D.D.
Henry R. Osgood	1957	D.D.
Clifford George Hansen	1958	D.D.
James Wesley Ingles	1958	D.D.
George Wendell Swope	1958	D.D.
L. Doward McBain	1959	D.D.
John Alphonso Molletti	1959	D.D.
William Prigger	1959	D.D.
Joseph H. Heartberg	1960	D.D.
Max W. Morgan	1960	D.D.
Gordon Palmer	1960	D.D.
Roy Gresham	1960	D.D.
C. Adrian Heaton	1960	D.D.
Thomas A. Buttimer	1961	D.D.
Stanley Nodder	1961	D.D.
John W. Taber	1961	D.D.
Laurence T. Beers	1962	D.D.
Franz Edward Oerth	1962	D.D.
George A. Cosper	1963	D.D.
Henry W. Habel	1963	D.D.
Edwin H. Frey	1964	D.D.
Edward B. Cole	1964	D.D.
R. Merrill Jensen	1965	D.D.
Chester J. Jump, Jr.	1965	D.D.
J. Wesley Rafter	1965	D.D.
Samuel A. Jeanes	1966	D.D.
J. Ithel Jones	1966	D.D.
Evan C. Pedrick	1966	D.D.
Everett C. Crimmings	1967	D.D.
W. Kenneth H. Ewing	1967	D.D.
W. Theodore Taylor	1967	D.D.
Harold Leroy Adams	1968	D.D.
John Elwood Bauers	1968	D.D.
William Edward Flood	1968	D.D.
Culbert G. Rutenber	1969	D.D.
Paul C. Allen	1969	D.D.
Floyd E. Brown	1969	D.D.
Harold Kenneth Heneise	1970	D.D.
Thomas Bruce McDormand	1970	D.D.
Oliver Ellsworth Peterson	1970	D.D.
Lloyd P. Frederick	1971	D.D.
William F. Keucher	1971	D.D.
Carl H. Morgan	1971	D.D.
R. Eugene Crow	1972	D.D.
John Hart Krier	1972	D.D.
Andre O. Buhika	1972	D.D.
B. Frank Belvin	1973	D.D.
Wilbert D. Gough	1973	D.D.
Wayne Nelson Hadley	1973	D.D.
Robert C. Campbell	1974	D.D.
Joseph R. Faith	1974	D.D.
Ralph R. Rott	1975	D.D.
Jane Gahs Wilson	1975	D.D.
W. Lowell Fairley	1976	D.D.

W. Everett Griffiths	1976	D.D.
John H. McKissick	1976	D.D.
Roger C. Palms	1977	D.D.
Russell G. Martin	1978	D.D.
Frank B. Mitchell, Jr.	1978	D.D.
Stacy D. Myers, Jr.	1978	D.D.
Richard E. Rusboldt	1979	D.D.
William L. Johnston	1980	D.D.
William H. Gray, III	1980	D.D.
Manuel C. Avila, Jr.	1981	D.D.
Rolando Gutierrez-Cortes	1981	D.D.
Calvin L. Moon	1982	D.D.
Robert W. Bouder	1983	D.D.
Albert Franklin Campbell	1984	D.D.
Santiago Soto Fontanez	1984	D.D.
Walter E. Fauntroy	1986	D.D.
Vinay K. Samuel	1986	D.D.
David B. Watermulder	1986	D.D.
Robert H. Roberts	1987	D.D.
Norman R. DePuy	1988	D.D.
Roland L. Johnson	1988	D.D.
Frederick W. Young	1988	D.D.
K. Imotemjen Aier	1989	D.D.
Godfrey Noel Vose	1989	D.D.
Heather Margaret Vose	1989	D.D.
Robert P. Meye	1990	D.D.
Lloyd H. Kenyon, Jr.	1991	D.D.
Denton Lotz	1991	D.D.
William Clair Krispin	1991	D.D.
Gus Roman	1992	D.D.
Oscar E. Remick	1993	D.D.
George Boltniew	1994	D.D.
Lawrence Taylor	1996	M.Div.
Suzan Johnson Cook	1996	D.D.
Patricia Shield Ayres	1997	D.D.
Alden A. Gaines	1997	D.D.
George Stuart Claghorn	1998	D.D.
G. Elaine Smith	1998	D.D.
William James Harvey III	1998	D.D.
Emmett Victor Johnson	1998	D.D.

SPEAKERS AT SEMINARY LECTURESHIPS

SWARTLEY

1956—Duke K. McCall	1980—Michael Green
1957—Browne Barr	1981—Rene Padilla
1958—Frank M. Kepner	1982—James Earl Massey
1960—J. Wesley Ingles	1983—Elizabeth Achtemeier
1961—Donald G. Miller	1984—James A. Forbes
1962—Rev. Robert G. Middleton	1985—Bryant M. Kirkland
1963—Dr. Harold John Ockenga	1986—David Watson
1964—Dr. Reginald Thomas	1987—Dennis Kinlaw
1966—Dr. Norman W. Paullin	1988—John Killenger
1967—Stephen F. Olford	1989—Charles G. Adams
1968—Dr. Lawrence L. Lacour	1990—William H. Canfield
1970—Gardner C. Taylor	1991—Suzan D. Johnson
1971—Edmund Steimle	1992—Henry H. Mitchell
1972—Edward V. Hill	1993—Thomas G. Long
1973—Eugene A. Nida	1994—James Earl Massey
1974—C. J. Oswald Hoffman	1995—Leonora Tubbs Tisdale
1975—Leighton Ford	1996—Raymond H. Bailey
1976—John R.W. Stott	1997—Paul Scott Wilson
1977—Helmut Thielicke	1998—William J. Harvey III
1978—Lloyd John Oglivie	1999—Eugene L. Lowrey
1979—Richard C. Halverson	

RUTENBER

1992—Jürgen Moltmann	1995—Cheryl J. Sanders
1993—Vinay and Colleen Samuel	1997—John H. Yoder
Melanie A. May	1999—David E. Goatley

TORBET

1991—Martin E. Marty	1996—Harry S. Stout
1992—Robert T. Handy	1998—Dana L. Robert
1994—Justo L. Gonzalez	

MITCHELL

1981—James H. Cone	1991—James E. Evans
1983—James Washington	1992—Wyatt Tee Walker
James Forbes	1993—Delores Carpenter
1984—Otis Moss	1994—William J. Shaw
1985—Joseph Lowery	1995—Jeremiah A. Wright, Jr.
1986—Gardner C. Taylor	1996—Floyd H. Flake
1987—Bernard Lafayette	1997—Gayraud S. Wilmore
Suzan Johnson	1998—John W. Kinney
1988—Miles J. Jones	1999—J. Deotis Roberts
1989—J. Alfred Smith	2000—Wallace Charles Smith
1990—Cain Hope Felder	

Index

Author's *epilogue*

According to the cliché, unless we study history we are doomed to repeat it. But sometimes we should study history because we ought to repeat it, or at least some aspects of it. Such is the case here.

A line in the Robert Anderson play *I Never Sang for My Father* reads, "Death ends a life, but not a relationship." In preparing this history, I experienced the truth of that statement. I found myself in a kind of relationship with people who were young and vibrant some seventy-five years ago. I got to know them—though not nearly so well as I would have liked—through their writings and through what was written and said about them.

The experience brought to mind a line from the Indigo Girls' song "Virginia Woolf," in which the songwriter tells of how she got to know and respect the famous author through her diary: "And here's a young girl on a kind of a telephone line through time. And the voice at the other end comes like a long-lost friend."

Across time, I developed an admiration and respect for the people who gave birth to Eastern Seminary, even though there were times when I wished I could yell at them for not doing a better job marking photos.

I have also thought about the words from the theme song of the 1996 Forward in Faithfulness campaign video. They express the hope that our children and their children someday, after we have lived our hopes and dreams, will sift through all we left behind and find evidence of faithfulness. The chorus begins: "O may all who come behind us find us faithful."

For this project, I have been the sifter. But the experience has made me keenly aware of how swiftly the sifters become the "siftees." One day, sooner than we realize, others will come along looking for evidence of faithfulness in our time. I hope and believe they will find it. To improve our chances, I'm definitely going back to mark a few photos.

About the *author*

Randall L. (Randy) Frame grew up in a small coal-mining town in Western Pennsylvania. Though he has not lived in Western Pennsylvania for two decades, his loyalties remain with the Pittsburgh Pirates, Steelers, and Penguins.

After receiving a B.A. degree from California University of Pennsylvania in English Literature, Frame went on to earn an M.A. in Communications from Wheaton (Illinois) College (1984). More recently he has taken courses at Eastern Seminary toward a Master of Theological Studies degree with a counseling emphasis.

His career in journalism began in earnest in October of 1982 when he became a news reporter and editor for *Christianity Today* magazine in Carol Stream, Illinois. His assignments for the magazine took him to thirty-one states and four foreign countries. They also enabled him to interview two of his "heroes": Fred Rogers (Mr. Rogers) and former President Jimmy Carter. After leaving Illinois in 1991, Frame maintained an association with *Christianity Today* as senior news writer, a part-time position, until 1998.

From 1991 till 1997, Frame served as director of communications at Eastern Seminary. Since August of 1997, he has served as acquisitions editor at Judson Press, the book publishing arm of the American Baptist Churches USA.

In addition to several hundred magazine and newspaper articles, Frame has written or co-written seven books, including *How Right Is the Right?* (Zondervan, 1996), in essence an appeal to fairness and moderation among Christians who are active in the political realm.

Frame's hobbies include creative writing, basketball, racquetball, and golf, even though he freely admits to having broken 100 only twice in some twenty years. He is also active as a girls soccer, basketball, and softball coach, and has appeared in various community theatre plays and musicals with one or more of his children.

Randy and wife, Jeron, who works in the Eastern Seminary library, reside in Paoli, Pennsylvania, with their three daughters: Annalyn (fifteen), Rennie (thirteen), and Marlise (ten).